TIM HARDY

GW00976215

NATURE QUEST

KINGFISHER

KINGFISHER

Kingfisher Publications Plc
New Penderel House
283–288 High Holborn
London WC1V 7HZ
www.kingfisherpub.com

First published by Kingfisher Publications Plc 2003
10 9 8 7 6 5 4 3 2 1

1TR/0603/POL/UNV-UP(UNV)/150MA

Copyright © Kingfisher Publications Plc 2003

All rights reserved. No part of this publication may
be reproduced, stored in a retrieval system or
transmitted by any means, electronic, mechanical,
photocopying or otherwise, without the prior
permission of the publisher.

A CIP catalogue record for this book is available
from the British Library.

ISBN 0 7534 0890 2

Printed in Slovakia

NATURE QUEST

Questions and Answers about the Natural World

KINGFISHER

Editors: Catherine Brereton, Carron Brown, Russell Mclean, Jennie Morris, Jonathan Stroud, Emma Wild

Designers: Catherine Goldsmith, John Jamieson, Malcolm Parchment

Consultants: Norah Granger, Chris Pellant, Joyce Pope, Claire Robinson, Stephen Savage

Production controller: Debbie Otter

DTP co-ordinators: Sarah Pfitzner, Nicky Studdart

Artwork archivists: Wendy Allison, Steve Robinson

Indexer: Chris Bernstein

Illustrators: Lisa Alderson 14–15, 22–23, 36–37, 42–43, 84–85, 88–89, 136–137; **Graham Allen** 126–127; **Robin Budden** 48–49; **Richard Draper** 74*tr*; **Chris Forsey** 56–57, 58–59, 68–69, 72–73, 72*bl*, 74–75, 80–81, 92–93, 94–95, 96–97, 98–99, 100–101, 132–133, 143*tl*, 146–147; **Craig Greenwood** 63*cr*, 63*tr*; **Ray Grinaway** 10–11, 16–17, 18–19, 54–55, 76–77, 120–121, 122–123, 134–135; **Ian Jackson** 20–21; **Terence Lambert** 78–79, 86–87; **Ruth Lindsay** 38–39, 44–45; **Kevin Maddison** 108–109; **Joannah May** 12–13, 24–25, 114–115, 116–117, 118–119, 142–143, 144–145; **Simon Mendez** 138–139; **Nicki Palin** 60–61*c*, 140–141; **Clive Pritchard** 144*bl*; **Bernard Robinson** 62–63*bl*; **Mike Rowe** 64–65, 104–105, 106–107; **Roger Stewart** 110–111; **Mike Taylor** 124–125, 128–129; **David Wright** 52–53, 66*bl*, 67*cl*, 82–83, 83*tr*.

Cartoons: Ian Dicks

Picture research managers: Jane Lambert, Cee Weston-Baker

Picture acknowledgements: 13*tl* Kjell B.Sandve/www.osf.uk.com; **19***tl* Isaac Kehimkar/www.osf.uk.com; **21***tl* Brian Bevan/Ardea London; **23***tr* R.J. Erwin/NHPA 1992; **25***tl* James Carmichael Jr./NHPA; **26***tl* Harald Lange/Bruce Coleman Collection; **33***cr* Ingrid N.Visser/Planet Earth Pictures; **41***tl* Fritz Polking/Still Pictures; **49***cr* Images Colour Library; **53***cr* Jean-Louis Le Moigne/NHPA; **55***cr* Z. Leszczynski/www.osf.uk.com; **59***tr* J.A.L. Cooke/www.osf.uk.com; **61***tr* Daniel Heuclin/NHPA; **65***cr* Martin Withers/Frank Lane Picture Agency; **77***tr* BBC Natural History Unit Picture Library/William Osborn; **78***cl* Ardea London/ Clem Haagner; **81***tl* www.osf.uk.com/Daniel J. Cox; **81***cr* BBC Natural History Unit Picture Library/Staffan Widstrand; **82***cl* NHPA/Stephen Dalton; **85***tr* BBC Natural History Unit Picture Library/Cindy Buxton; **87***tr* NHPA/Bill Coster; **89***bl* NHPA/Mike Lane; **95***tl* NHPA/Daniel Heuchlin; **95***cr* Science Photo Library/Matthew Oldfield, Scubazoo; **96***bl* Corbis/Tony Arruza; **99***tr* Corbis/Lawson Wood; **100***bl* NHPA/Ant Photo Library; **102***bl* NHPA/B. Jones & M. Shimlock; **105***bl* Trevor McDonald/NHPA; **119***tr* M. Watson/Ardea London; **122***tr* Kjell Sandved/ www.osf.uk.com; **123***tl* John Marsh/Ardea London; **132***cl* Martin Harvey/NHPA; **137***cr* Bruce Coleman Collection; **138***cl* Jurgen & Christine Sohns/Frank Lane Picture Agency; **147***tr* Silvestris/Frank Lane Picture Agency.

Every effort has been made to trace the copyright holders of the photographs. The publishers apologise for any inconvenience caused.

CONTENTS

ABOUT this book

Have you ever wondered what creepy–crawlies eat, what a kangaroo keeps in its pouch or what lives in a rock pool? This book will give you the answer to these questions – and hundreds more. On every page, find out the answers to questions like this and other fascinating facts about the natural world. Words in **bold** are explained in the glossary on pages 149-155.

Look and Find
★ stonefish ★

All through the book, you will see the Look and Find symbol. This has the name and picture of a small object that is hidden somewhere on the page. Look carefully to see if you can find it.

Now I know...

★ This box contains quick answers to all of the questions.

★ They will help you remember all about the amazing natural world.

Creepy-crawlies

Jim Bruce

★ Look and Find ★
caterpillar

WHAT are creepy-crawlies?

Creepy-crawlies are tiny creatures that buzz, scuttle, wriggle and creep all around us. Creepy-crawlies include **insects**, spiders, millipedes, worms, woodlice, slugs and snails. They vary in size, shape and colour, but they are all **invertebrates**. This means they have no backbone.

WHERE do they live?

Creepy-crawlies are found almost everywhere on earth. Every garden is home to thousands of them. They are so small that they can squeeze into the tiniest of spaces and can be very hard to spot. Creepy-crawlies hide in dark, damp places, such as under stones, leaves and logs, and in the soil. Some are busy during the day, but others come out only at night.

HOW many creepy-crawlies are there?

There are more creepy-crawlies in the world than any other kind of animal – over three million **species**. In fact, there are so many different kinds that scientists have sorted them into groups. For example, bees, ants and dragonflies are insects, spiders and scorpions are **arachnids**, and snails and slugs are **molluscs**.

That's Amazing!

The first flight on earth was not made by a bird, but by an insect – over 400 million years ago!

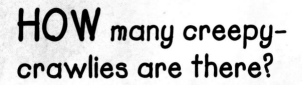

All sorts of creepy-crawlies are hiding in the long grass. Look out for them throughout the book.

Now I Know...

★ Creepy-crawlies are small creatures without backbones.
★ Creepy-crawlies live almost everywhere on earth.
★ There are over three million kinds of creepy-crawly.

WHY do insects wear armour?

★ Look and Find ★
greenfly

All insects have a hard casing on the outside of their body called an **exoskeleton**. Just like a strong suit of armour, this protects their soft insides. All insects have three parts to their bodies. The front part, the head, holds the brain, mouth, eyes and **antennae**. The middle part, the **thorax**, carries three pairs of legs and usually contains the wings. The back part, the **abdomen**, contains the stomach. In female insects, this is where the eggs are made.

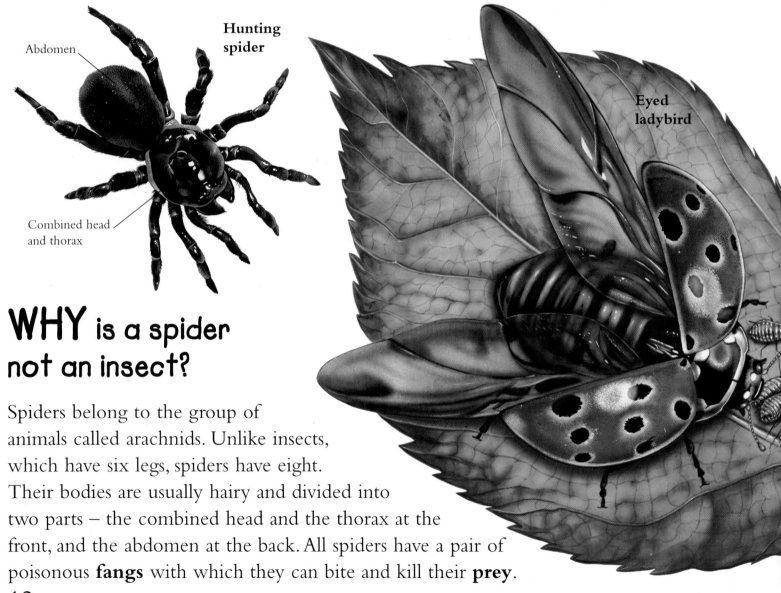

Abdomen

Hunting spider

Combined head and thorax

Eyed ladybird

WHY is a spider not an insect?

Spiders belong to the group of animals called arachnids. Unlike insects, which have six legs, spiders have eight. Their bodies are usually hairy and divided into two parts – the combined head and the thorax at the front, and the abdomen at the back. All spiders have a pair of poisonous **fangs** with which they can bite and kill their **prey**.

12

HOW do insects see?

Many animals have only one lens in each eye, but insects such as dragonflies and horse flies have **compound eyes**. Their eyes are made up of thousands of tiny lenses packed together. This kind of eye does not see objects clearly, but it does allow the insects to spot even the slightest movement from almost any direction.

That's Amazing!

When it is very cold, some insects produce special chemicals that stop their blood turning to ice!

Creepy-crawlies have different coloured blood to other animals – it is green or yellow!

Seven spot ladybird

All creepy-crawlies, including ladybirds, have similar parts on the inside. They have nerves which carry signals from one part of their body to another, and they breathe using tiny air pipes called **tracheae**.

Now I Know...

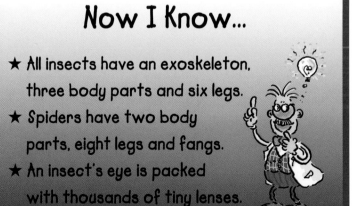

★ All insects have an exoskeleton, three body parts and six legs.
★ Spiders have two body parts, eight legs and fangs.
★ An insect's eye is packed with thousands of tiny lenses.

13

HOW do caterpillars grow up?

A wriggling caterpillar and a colourful, fluttering butterfly look very different. In fact, they are actually the same insect at different stages of life. Every young caterpillar will change its shape, size and colour before it becomes an adult butterfly. This is called **metamorphosis**.

1 Female butterflies lay eggs on plants that will provide the young caterpillars with the type of food they eat.

2 When the eggs **hatch**, the caterpillars immediately start to eat and grow quickly.

3 When fully grown, the caterpillars become **pupae**. They make a special shell in which their bodies begin to change.

4 After some time, the shell splits open and a new adult butterfly wriggles free.

A swallowtail caterpillar feeding

That's Amazing!

Some fully-grown caterpillars can weigh up to 2,700 times more than they did at birth!

Thirsty butterflies sip the juice of rotten fruit that contains alcohol!

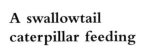

Although most caterpillars have twelve eyes, their eyesight is still very poor. They can only tell the difference between light and dark. Some caterpillars have no eyes at all, and get around by using touch and smell alone.

14

WHAT do butterflies eat?

Adult butterflies do not need much food, but they do need sugars, such as **nectar**, for energy. Brightly-coloured flowers contain this liquid. The butterflies unroll their long tongues, and suck up sticky nectar from inside the flowers. When they are thirsty, they drink water from ponds and streams.

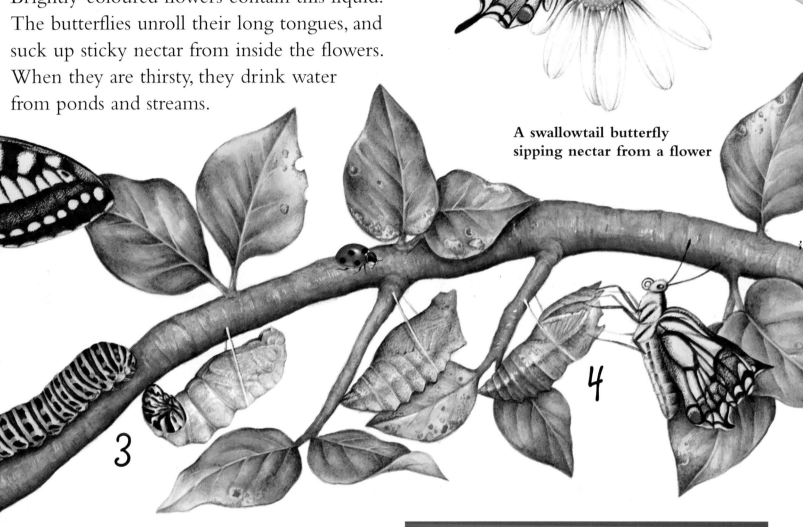

A swallowtail butterfly sipping nectar from a flower

3

4

WHERE do butterflies go to sleep?

At night-time and in bad weather, butterflies find a quiet place to sleep, on the underside of twigs and leaves, or on the top of a blade of grass. They often rest in the same place night after night.

Now I Know...

★ Caterpillars change a lot before they become butterflies.
★ Nectar is a sweet, sticky fluid that butterflies eat.
★ Butterflies often sleep in the same place every night.

★ Look and Find ★
woodlouse

WHAT do creepy-crawlies eat?

The dark woodland floor is an ideal place for creepy-crawlies, providing food and shelter. There are plenty of plants to nibble on or hide under, and lots of tiny animals to catch. Worms, snails, millipedes and woodlice feed on the rotting remains of plants as well as leaves, fruits and seeds. In turn, these plant-eating creepy-crawlies are food for ferocious woodland hunters such as spiders and beetles.

WHY do stag beetles have big jaws?

Many beetles have powerful jaws for grabbing, biting and chewing their prey. Male stag beetles have large jaws shaped like a pair of antlers. During the breeding season, they use them to wrestle with rival males, sometimes lifting them off the ground.

Plant-eaters and hunters feeding

Male stag beetles

Millipede

Millipede

Earthworm

Woodlouse

That's Amazing!

Flies eat all sorts of strange things. Some have even been known to eat shoe polish – *yum!*

More trees are destroyed by insects each year than are burned down in forest fires!

Long-horn beetle

Tiger beetle

Female stag beetle

Ant

HOW do worms help plants to grow?

Earthworms are some of the most useful animals on earth. As they crawl and eat their way through the soil, they mix in dead animals and plants. This feeds the soil, and helps new plants to grow. Earthworms have long, soft bodies and no legs.

Now I Know...

★ Creepy-crawlies eat rotting remains, plants or small animals.
★ Male stag beetles have powerful jaws for fighting.
★ Earthworms mix dead plants and animals into the soil.

Look and Find ★ snail

WHY do glow-worms glow?

Glow-worms are not actually worms, but small beetles. To attract a **mate**, the females give out a bright light made by chemicals in an organ on the underside of their abdomens. Female glow-worms have no wings and have to climb to the top of blades of grass to signal to flying males. Fireflies are close relatives of glow-worms. Both male and female give out a yellowish glow.

WHY do grasshoppers 'sing'?

Grasshoppers use sound to attract mates and warn rivals. The males 'sing' by scraping their back legs against a vein in their front wings, like a violin player drawing a bow across a string. Each species has its own special tune.

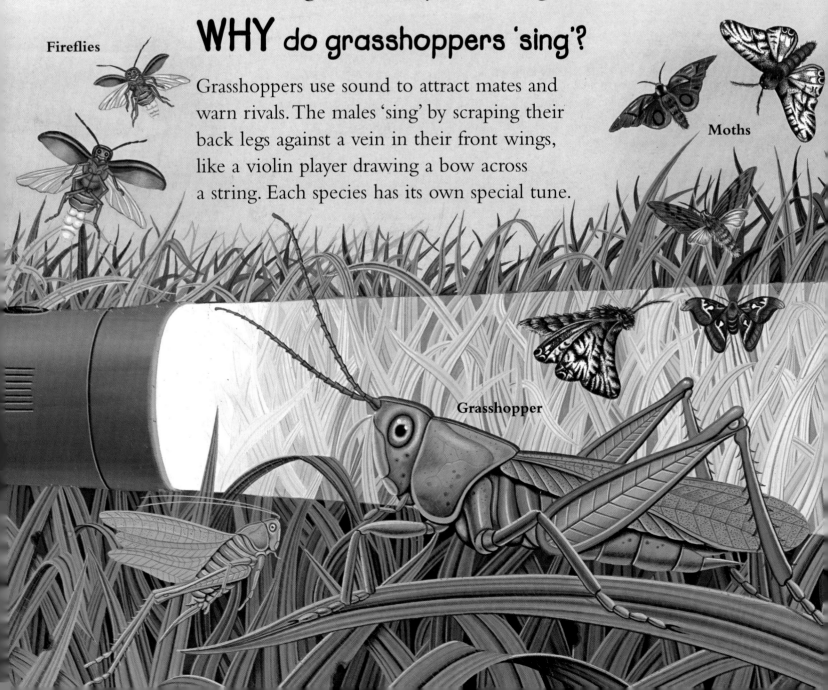

Fireflies

Moths

Grasshopper

WHICH insect is noisiest?

The noisiest insect in the world is the cicada. Males spend a lot of time in trees where they 'chirrup' loudly using two plates on the side of their abdomen. They can be heard over 400 metres away – about the distance of four football pitches.

That's Amazing!

A South American firefly, the railway worm, got its name because it flashes red and green like a railway signal!

Some insects hear sounds using the delicate hairs on their antennae!

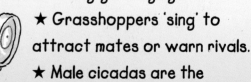

Summer nights are filled with all kinds of insects sending messages to each other using light and sound.

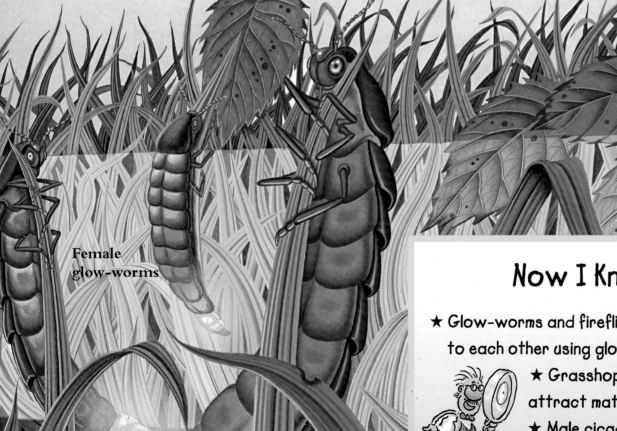

Female glow-worms

Snail

Now I Know...

★ Glow-worms and fireflies send messages to each other using glowing light.

★ Grasshoppers 'sing' to attract mates or warn rivals.

★ Male cicadas are the noisiest insects – ever!

WHY do grasshoppers lose their skin?

Female grasshoppers lay eggs. The newborn insects that hatch out are called **nymphs**. They look like tiny copies of their parents, but without wings. Grasshoppers grow in stages. As the nymphs grow bigger, their outer skin becomes too small and they wriggle out. This is called **moulting**. The insects then grow before their new skin hardens.

HOW many eggs do insects lay?

Female grasshoppers lay as few as two, or as many as 120 eggs at a time, though some insects can lay thousands. Egg shells keep the young warm, moist and hidden. Insects often leave their eggs on or near food that the young insects will eat after they hatch.

Young grasshopper

Female grasshoppers often lay their eggs in sandy soil. After they hatch, the young grasshoppers dig their way out to the surface.

Grasshopper eggs

Grasshopper nymph

One kind of grasshopper, called a locust, can gather in huge groups of up to 250,000 million insects!

WHAT grows in a bag?

To keep their babies safe, some spiders wrap their eggs in a home-made silk bag called a sac. Some hang this sac on their webs, while others carry it around on their backs. Young spiders, called **spiderlings**, hatch inside the egg sac. They leave after their first moult, when they are able to spin silk.

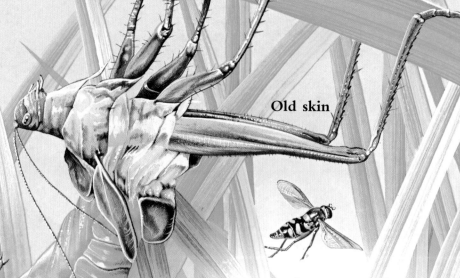

Old skin

Final moult

A young grasshopper moults five or six times before it becomes an adult. On the final moult, it has full-length wings.

Now I Know...

★ When they are born, grasshoppers look like tiny copies of their parents.
★ Most insects lay a lot of eggs, usually near a food source.
★ Some spiders wrap their eggs in a silk bag called a sac.

21

WHY do spiders spin webs?

Some spiders use sticky traps to help them catch food. They spin fine webs, using silk made in special **glands** in their bodies. The silk is liquid inside the spider, but hardens into a strong thread outside its body. When an insect becomes tangled in the web, the spider feels it struggling through hairs on its legs, and rushes over to kill it.

**Garden
cross spider**

Web-spinning spiders never get caught in their own webs. They have special greasy feet that slip easily along the silk lines.

WHAT shape is an orb-web spider's web?

Orb-web spiders weave their round webs in open areas, often between tree branches or flower stems. Some spiders lie in wait close by for insects to get caught. Others hold a thread of silk, called a trap line, attached to the centre of the web, and hide nearby. When an insect lands in the web, the line vibrates and the spider darts out to attack it.

22

Some spiders wrap up their captured victims in silk, so they cannot escape. Later, they return to the web to eat the insects.

That's Amazing!

Some spiders spin a new web every night. They are experts, so it takes only one hour!

Spider silk is thinner than a hair, but it is stronger than steel wire of the same thickness!

WHERE do some baby spiders live?

Some spiders do not spin webs to catch other animals, but use them instead as 'nurseries' to protect their young. The spiders guard their eggs until the tiny spiderlings are ready to spill out – usually after the babies' second moult. These webs are usually build in plants or shrubs.

Nursery web spider

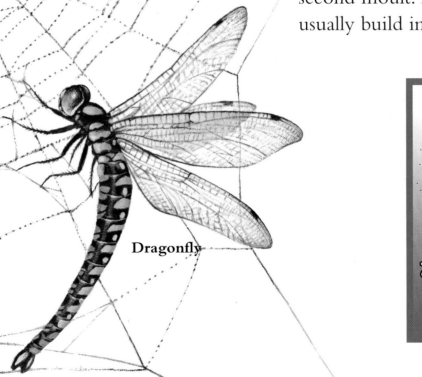

Dragonfly

Now I Know...

★ Spiders use their fine, sticky webs to capture their prey.
★ Orb-web spiders spin round webs made from silk.
★ Some spiders look after their young in 'nursery' webs.

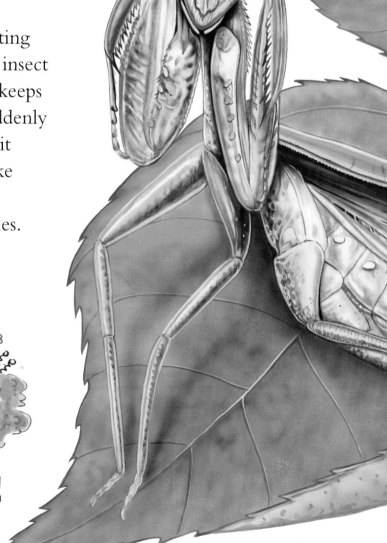

Praying
mantis

WHICH insect looks like a twig?

Look and Find
beetle

All creepy-crawlies have enemies that want to eat them. Some stay alive by disguising themselves as something that is not worth eating. Others blend cleverly into their **habitats**. Stick insects have bodies that look like twigs, while leaf insects look like bright green leaves. Some caterpillars even look like birds' droppings. Other creatures contain poison or bad-tasting chemicals that make them impossible to eat.

WHY does a mantis pray?

A mantis holds its front legs together while waiting to attack, so that it looks like it is praying. If an insect lands nearby, the mantis stays perfectly still, but keeps watch by swivelling its head slightly. Then it suddenly strikes. Its front legs snap around its victim and it begins to feed immediately. The mantis' stick-like green body blends into the surrounding leaves. This helps it to stay hidden from hungry enemies.

That's Amazing!

The bombardier beetle shoots its enemies with a cloud of hot, stinging liquid!

The longest insect is the tropical stick insect which reaches 35 cm!

24

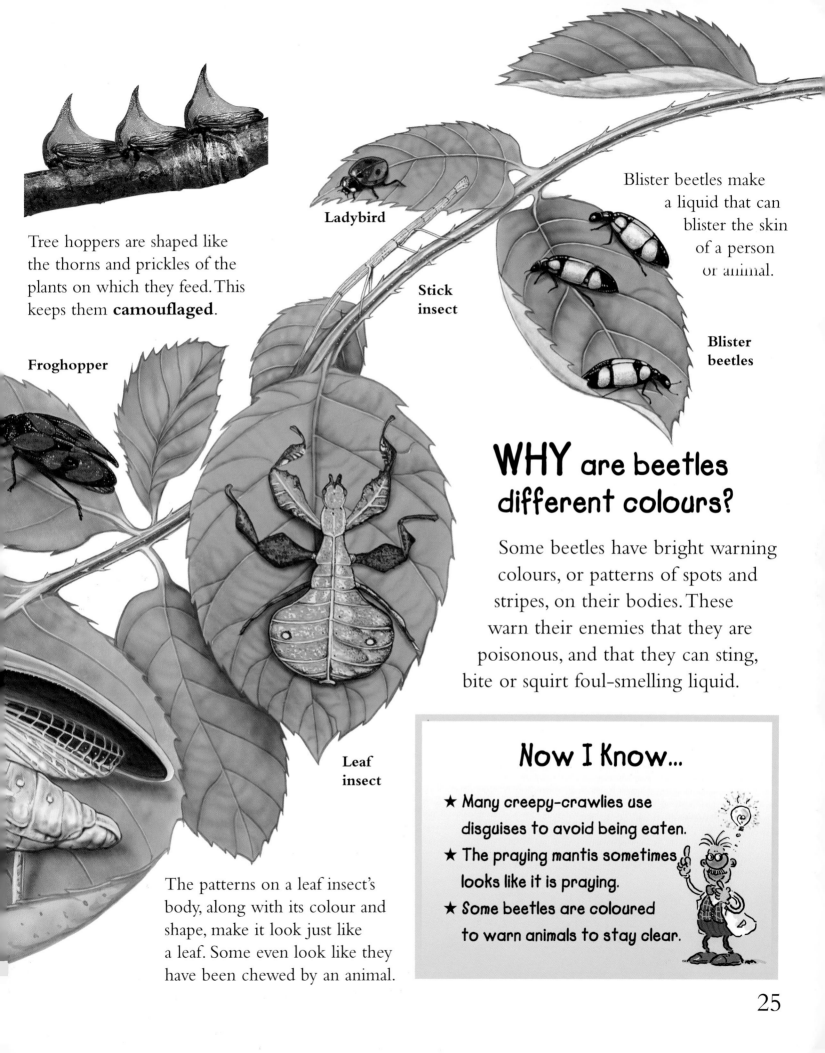

Tree hoppers are shaped like the thorns and prickles of the plants on which they feed. This keeps them **camouflaged**.

Froghopper

Ladybird

Stick insect

Blister beetles make a liquid that can blister the skin of a person or animal.

Blister beetles

Leaf insect

The patterns on a leaf insect's body, along with its colour and shape, make it look just like a leaf. Some even look like they have been chewed by an animal.

WHY are beetles different colours?

Some beetles have bright warning colours, or patterns of spots and stripes, on their bodies. These warn their enemies that they are poisonous, and that they can sting, bite or squirt foul-smelling liquid.

Now I Know...

★ Many creepy-crawlies use disguises to avoid being eaten.
★ The praying mantis sometimes looks like it is praying.
★ Some beetles are coloured to warn animals to stay clear.

25

★ Look and Find ★

spider

WHY do ants live together?

Ants are social insects, like bees and termites. They live and work together in large, organized groups called **colonies**. Each nest contains a single queen, which lays all the eggs. Most of the other ants are female workers. They build the home, search for food, keep the nest clean, fight enemies and look after the young **larvae**.

Termites are amazing colony builders. They make mud nests up to four times the height of an adult human.

Wood ants in their nest

Larvae

That's Amazing!

When ants find food, they mark a smelly trail to their nest, so others can follow!

Tiny ants can lift objects more than 20 times their own weight!

26

WHICH ants are like storage jars?

Honeypot ants use certain worker ants as 'storage jars' to hold plant juices. In the summer, when food is plentiful, these ants are fed nectar and honeydew by the other workers. They swell up like balloons, and hang upside down in the nest. When food supplies are low, the workers tap them with their antennae to make them release food.

Honeypot ants

HOW do ants make their treetop tents?

Weaver ants 'sew' leaves together to make tents in the treetops, using their young like a needle and thread. Each ant holds a larva in its mouth, and pokes it against the edges of the leaves. The larva makes a sticky thread that binds the leaves together.

Weaver ants

Female worker ants searching for food

Now I Know...

★ The queen ant is the most important member of the nest.
★ Some honeypot ants store tasty food in their bodies.
★ Weaver ants use their larvae like a needle and thread.

A queen laying eggs

27

CREEPY-CRAWLIES QUIZ

What have you remembered about creepy-crawlies? Test your knowledge and see how much you have learned.

1 What sort of animal is a ladybird?
a) spider
b) mollusc
c) insect

2 What do butterflies eat?
a) nectar
b) other insects
c) honey

3 Where do grasshoppers lay their eggs?
a) in a pond
b) in the air
c) underground

4 How many legs do spiders have?
a) four
b) six
c) eight

5 From what is a spider's web made?
a) plants
b) wood
c) silk

6 What are baby grasshoppers called?
a) nymphs
b) spiderlings
c) larvae

7 Which sort of ant lays eggs?
a) queen
b) worker
c) larva

8 Which creepy-crawly gives out a bright light?
a) earthworm
b) glow-worm
c) ant

9 What do tree hoppers look like?
a) leaves
b) thorns
c) sticks

10 Which creepy-crawly is the noisiest?
a) butterfly
b) cicada
c) bee

Find the answers on page 160.

Mammals

Jim Bruce

★ Look and Find ★
snail

WHAT is a mammal?

Although mice, bats, giraffes, leopards and whales may seem very different, they all belong to a group of animals called mammals. Mammals are animals that have special things in common. They are **warm-blooded**, have fur or body hair, and have bony skeletons that support their bodies. Most mammals give birth to live young, and the mothers feed their young on their milk. All these things are true about us, so humans are mammals too.

Giraffes feeding and drinking

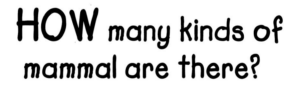

Mother leopard with cub

HOW many kinds of mammal are there?

There are at least 4,300 different species, or kinds, of mammal. Sometimes, a new species of mammal is discovered, but there are probably no more than a few new species left to be found.

Harvest mouse

That's Amazing!

Humans live longer than any other mammal – a few have lived for more than 120 years!

Mammals are the most intelligent of all the animals and have extra-large brains!

HOW big do mammals grow?

Mammals come in all shapes and sizes, from tiny to very large. About half of all known mammals are small **rodents**, such as squirrels and mice, and about one quarter are bats. Some mammals, such as elephants, whales and lions, grow to be very large. The sea-living blue whale is the biggest mammal of all, and weighs more than 150 tonnes. The largest land mammal is the African elephant, which can weigh up to eight tonnes.

Although human babies are bigger than many fully grown mammals, they are completely helpless. They need their parents to look after them for many years.

Now I know...

★ Mammals may look very different, but they have many things in common.
★ More than 4,300 different species of mammal exist.
★ Some mammals grow to be very large, but most are quite small.

31

HOW do polar bears keep warm?

Like all mammals, polar bears are warm-blooded animals. Their bodies stay at the same temperature whether the air or water around them is hot or cold. Most mammals are also covered in hair. Polar bears have a very thick coat to keep out the freezing cold of the **Arctic**. In winter, they also shelter in a **den**, or hole, which they dig in the snow.

WHY is a polar bear white?

As well as to keep it warm, a polar bear has a white coat to **camouflage** it against the snow when it hunts for food. In fact, its whole body is perfect for life in its surroundings. Its large paws are excellent snow-shoes as well as great paddles for swimming.

That's Amazing!

Polar bears do not need to drink. They get all their liquid from the food they eat!

Polar bears can swim for 100 km without stopping!

Polar bear

WHAT makes a walrus fat?

Under its skin, a walrus has a thick layer of fat called **blubber**. This keeps it warm in the icy waters of the Arctic. Other Arctic mammals, such as polar bears and seals, also have this layer of fat to protect them from the cold. A walrus has two long, sharp tusks, which it uses to dig up shellfish and crabs from the seabed. The tusks are also used as weapons when fighting.

Seal

To stay fat and warm, Arctic mammals must eat a lot of food. A polar bear eats seals, fish, seabirds and walruses, plus plants and berries in the summer. Polar bears have an amazing sense of smell. They can sniff out a live seal one metre under the ice.

Now I know...

★ All mammals are warm-blooded.
★ A polar bear's white coat camouflages it against the snow.
★ Blubber is a layer of fat under Arctic mammals' skin that keeps them warm.

WHY are whales such whoppers?

Larger than any dinosaur, the blue whale is the biggest animal that has ever lived. An adult can grow up to 33 metres long, the same length as a jumbo jet. It can weigh more than 150 tonnes, which is as heavy as 30 elephants. The blue whale is able to grow so huge because its giant body is always supported by the water around it. Whales are powerful swimmers. Some can even leap out of the water.

WHAT is a blowhole?

Sea-living mammals, such as whales and dolphins, cannot breathe underwater like fish. They must come to the surface for air. They breathe in and out through a **blowhole**. This is the nostril or breathing-hole on the top of the head. When they let out the used air, they send out a spray of water called a spout.

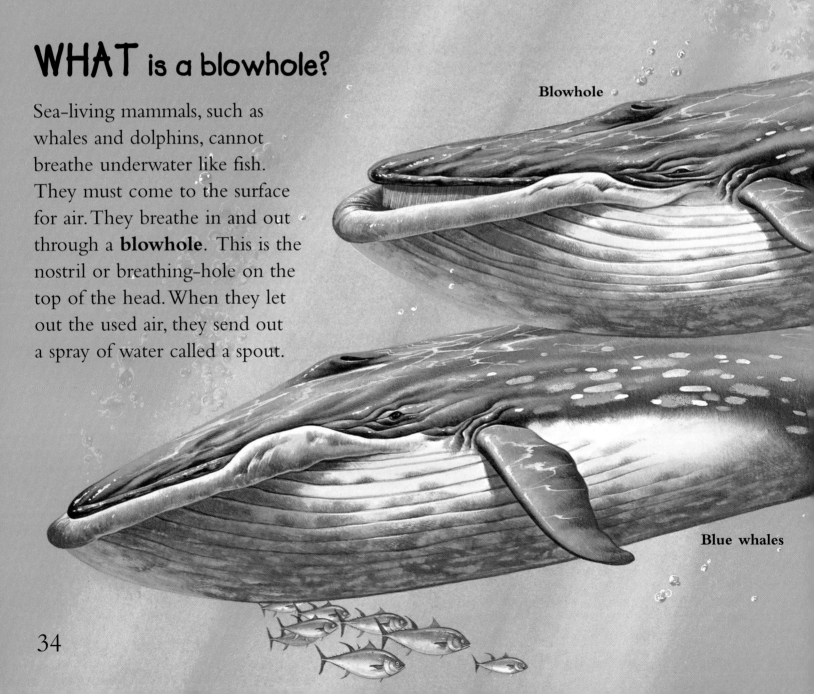

Blowhole

Blue whales

34

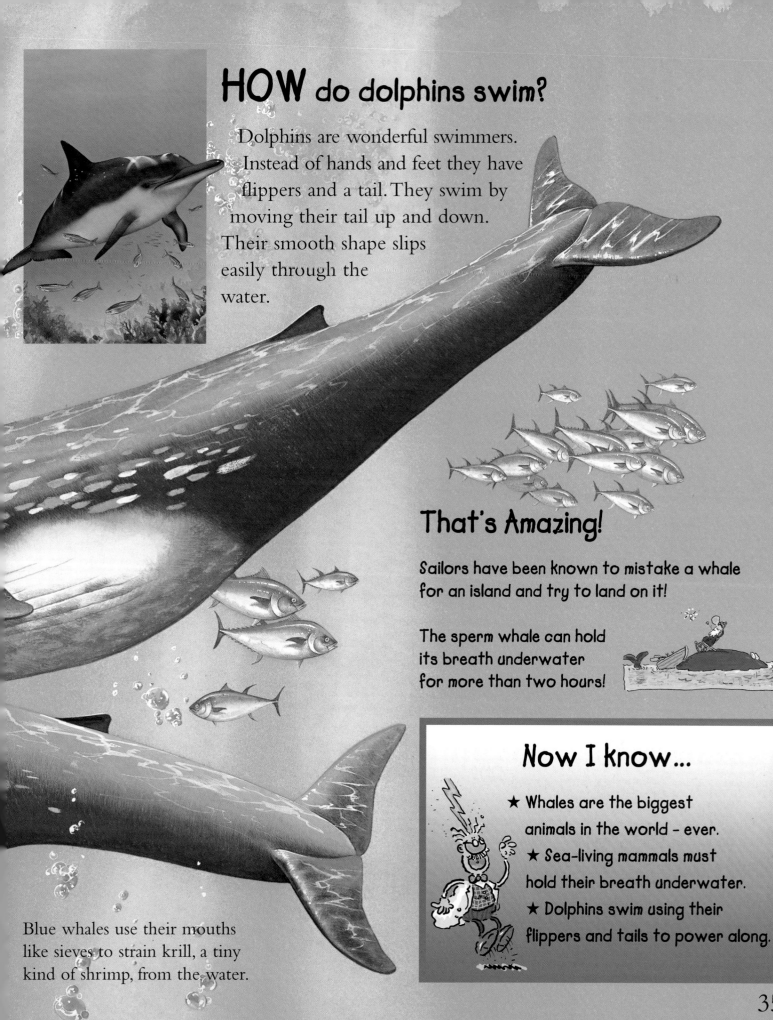

HOW do dolphins swim?

Dolphins are wonderful swimmers. Instead of hands and feet they have flippers and a tail. They swim by moving their tail up and down. Their smooth shape slips easily through the water.

That's Amazing!

Sailors have been known to mistake a whale for an island and try to land on it!

The sperm whale can hold its breath underwater for more than two hours!

Now I know...

★ Whales are the biggest animals in the world - ever.
★ Sea-living mammals must hold their breath underwater.
★ Dolphins swim using their flippers and tails to power along.

Blue whales use their mouths like sieves to strain krill, a tiny kind of shrimp, from the water.

WHICH mammals can fly?

Look and Find ★ caterpillar

Bats are the only mammals that can truly fly. Like birds, they have light bodies, but they have no feathers. Their wings are layers of skin stretched between long finger bones. Bats are **nocturnal** and sleep during the day. They hang upside down from cave roofs or tree branches. As the sun sets, they fly into the night in search of food.

Flying fox bat

HOW do bats find food in the dark?

Most bats have poor sight. While hunting at night, they send out high-pitched squeaks that bounce off objects and return to the bats' ears as echoes. This is called **echolocation**. From these sounds, the bats can tell where things are – such as tasty insects.

Kitti's hog-nosed bat

This minute bat is one of the world's smallest mammals. It is about the size of a bumble bee and weighs no more than two grammes.

That's Amazing!

One type of insect-eating bat can eat 600 mosquitoes in an hour!

Sometimes, millions of bats live together in a huge group called a colony!

WHY do sugar gliders leap from trees?

The Australian sugar glider leaps from the treetops to find food or to escape from enemies. Although it has no wings, it has a thin, furry skin that stretches along its body. This helps it to **glide** from tree to tree, like a paper dart. It can travel 50 metres in one jump.

Most bats are **insectivores** – they eat only insects. But some bats, such as the flying fox, feed on fruits.

Now I know...

★ Bats have wings and are the only mammals that can fly like birds.

★ Sugar gliders cannot fly, but glide from tree to tree.

★ Most bats hunt during the night using their excellent hearing.

WHAT do hippos eat?

Like many other mammals, the hippopotamus is a vegetarian and eats only plants. Mammal plant-eaters are called **herbivores**. They have strong teeth to help them grind up their tough food, and special stomachs to digest it. To get all the energy they need, they have to spend many hours every day feeding.

WHICH mammals chew and chew?

Hoofed mammals, such as buffaloes, giraffes and antelopes, feed mainly on grass and leaves. As their diet is so tough, they munch their food twice. After grabbing a big mouthful, they quickly swallow it after one chew. The food goes into their stomachs, but comes back up for a second chew after it has become softer.

Elephants

Buffaloes

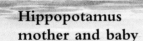

Hippopotamus mother and baby

A hippo bathing

Because they all eat a range of different foods, many plant-eaters can live in the same area. In the evening when the sun has set, many herbivores go to the local waterhole to feed.

WHY do giraffes have long necks and legs?

The world's tallest mammal is the giraffe. It can be as tall as five metres. It gets its great height from its very long neck and legs. Being so tall, giraffes can stretch right up into the trees to pull off juicy leaves and shoots that other animals cannot reach. Even though its neck is long, a giraffe has only seven neck bones – the same number as all other mammals.

Giraffes eating acacia leaves

Antelope

Zebras drinking at a waterhole

Some mammals, such as humans, can eat plants and meat. They are called **omnivores**.

That's Amazing!

As well as being the tallest mammal, a giraffe also has a huge tongue - more than 45 cm in length!

Hippos are very large animals - no wonder - they eat about 60 kg of plants every day!

Now I know...

★ Many mammals, such as hippos and giraffes, are plant-eaters.

★ Herbivores chew their food over and over again.

★ Giraffes have long necks and legs, so they can reach treetops.

Look and Find grasshopper

WHERE do lions catch their dinner?

Mammals that are meat-eaters, such as lions, tigers and cheetahs, are called **carnivores**. Big cats are built to hunt, and have powerful bodies, sharp eyesight and a good sense of smell. Lions live in family groups called **prides**. They hunt their prey on the plains and in the woodlands of Africa. The females of the group do most of the hunting, but the males soon arrive to make sure they get their share of the feast.

That's Amazing!

Cheetahs love making lots of noise - they are always chirping, purring, humming and yelping!

Unlike most cats, tigers are very fond of water, and are strong swimmers!

A lion can eat 23 kg of meat in one meal - that's the same as more than 250 beefburgers!

WHAT is the fastest mammal?

The cheetah is the fastest mammal. It can run at a top speed of 110 kilometres per hour, but only in short bursts. Unlike most cats, its claws stick out all the time, helping it to grip the ground as it runs.

Two lionesses chase an antelope

WHY do tigers have stripes?

Tigers are easy to recognize, with thick black stripes covering their orange body. These markings help them blend in with the light and shade of the forest. They can creep up quickly and quietly on their prey without being spotted, especially at sunset when they like to hunt.

Now I know...

★ Carnivores, such as the big hunting cats, eat only meat.
★ The fastest mammal in the world is the speedy cheetah.
★ A tiger's stripes help to keep it hidden in the forest.

41

HOW do beavers build their home?

Many mammals build homes to shelter their young. A whole beaver family helps to build a **lodge** in the river. This structure is made from logs, branches and rocks stuck together with mud. The beavers cut the logs by gnawing through trees with their sharp teeth. Inside the lodge is an area above water that is warm and dry even in bad weather. Here, the beavers can bring up their young in safety.

Beaver

WHY do dormice need a nest?

Dormice have nests to keep them snug and protected. During the cold winter, they spend several months asleep, or **hibernating**. The hibernating animal's body slows down and its heart beats less often. It does not eat and lives off fat stored in its body.

That's Amazing!

Beavers build canals more than 200 m long to make quick routes from one river to another!

More than 400 million prairie dogs lived in one underground town in Texas in the U.S.A.!

WHERE do prairie dogs live?

A prairie dog is a type of rodent living in North America. Family groups dig underground **burrows**. These are linked together by tunnels to make towns for hundreds of prairie dogs. Some act as sentries and keep watch above ground for enemies.

Lodge

Now I know...

★ Beavers live in wooden lodges on the river that are built by all the family.

★ In the winter, hibernating animals keep warm in nests.

★ Prairie dogs live in burrows that link to make vast towns.

Look and Find

toad

WHEN do elephants stop growing?

When they are born, most mammal babies are blind and helpless, but newborn elephant calves can walk when they are just one hour old. Unlike other young, they never completely stop growing. The older they get, the larger they grow. Female elephants will stay with their mothers and relatives in the same herd long after they become adults.

HOW do young mammals learn?

Mammals give their young more protection and training than other animals do. Young mammals learn many skills from their mothers, such as finding food and keeping out of danger. Sometimes, the father also cares for the young. He protects them from enemy attack, and helps to find food for them.

44

That's Amazing!

When it is born, a baby elephant weighs 145 kg – more than twice the weight of an adult human!

The Asian elephant is pregnant for 609 days – over two and a half times as long as a human!

WHAT do piglets eat?

For their first few weeks, a mother pig feeds her piglets on her milk. Mammals are the only animals that do this. Some mammals, such as elephants, feed milk to their young until they are several years old.

A young elephant is protected by the females in the herd

Elephants love bathing. They are very good swimmers, and can give themselves a shower by squirting water through their trunks.

Now I know...

★ Elephants are so huge because they do not stop growing – ever.

★ Mammal mothers teach their babies survival skills.

★ Piglets, like all mammals, feed on their mother's milk.

45

WHAT does a kangaroo keep in its pouch?

Kangaroos belong to a group of mammals called **marsupials**. Marsupial mothers have a pouch on the front of their stomachs. When a baby kangaroo, or joey, is born, it is only about two centimetres long. It is too tiny to survive in the outside world, so it crawls up into its mother's warm pouch. Once there, the baby drinks milk and grows bigger. After eight months, it is large enough to leave the pouch safely.

Like most marsupials, kangaroos are only found in the wild in Australia.

That's Amazing!

The leaves that koalas eat contain strong-smelling oils that keep bugs away!

A platypus finds food in the mud using special electric sensors inside its bill!

Female red kangaroo with her joey

46

WHY do koalas love to sleep and sleep?

Koalas are expert climbers, and spend most of their time in eucalyptus trees, eating the young shoots. Their leafy diet does not give them much energy, so they sleep for up to 18 hours a day. They only become active at night when it is time to eat again.

WHICH mammals lay leathery eggs?

Two mammals, the platypus and the echidna (a spiny anteater), do not give birth to live young. Instead, they lay eggs that are protected by leathery shells. After laying her eggs in a nest, the mother platypus warms them with her body for about ten days until they hatch. Mammals that lay eggs are called **monotremes**.

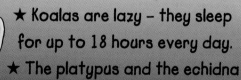

Now I know...

★ A female kangaroo has a pouch, so that her baby has a safe place to grow.

★ Koalas are lazy – they sleep for up to 18 hours every day.

★ The platypus and the echidna are the only mammals that lay eggs.

Look and Find ★ ★ snake

WHY do chimps chatter?

Almost all mammals have some way of **communicating** with animals of their own kind. Chimpanzees communicate, or 'chatter', using sounds and signs. They bark, pant or grunt, to tell others when food is found. They hoot loudly and beat on tree-trunks to warn when enemies are nearby. Chimps often greet each other with hugs and kisses, just like humans.

That's Amazing!

Scientists have found that chimps treat themselves for illness using plants from the forest as medicines!

Wild chimps use leaves as sponges to soak up water to drink!

Young chimpanzee

WHAT does a dog's bark mean?

Dogs bark at other animals to tell them where their **territory** is. An animal's territory is the area that it moves around and where it feeds. A pet dog's territory may be around its owner's house. Dogs will also bark if they are excited, or just want to say 'hello'.

Sheep dog

48

WHICH mammals love to 'talk'?

Like other intelligent mammals, dolphins are playful and communicative. They live in groups called schools, and 'talk' to each other using clicks and whistles. These sounds travel under the water for many kilometres. Scientists also think that dolphins can copy human speech, but at a much faster rate.

A chimp communicates with its group

Chimps spend a lot of their time in trees. They use their strong arms to swing from branch to branch in search of food. At night, they build treetop nests from leaves and sleep in them.

Now I know...

★ Chimps send messages to each other using sounds and signs.

★ A dog's bark can mean 'hello' or 'keep away please!'.

★ Dolphins are intelligent and 'talk' to each other.

MAMMALS QUIZ

What have you remembered about mammals? Test what you know and see how much you have learned.

1 What kind of mammal is a prairie dog?
a)   cat
b)   rodent
c)   dog

2 Which mammal has blubber?
a)   mouse
b)   chimp
c)   walrus

3 Which mammal eats only plants?
a)   giraffe
b)   lion
c)   polar bear

4 Which mammal lives in a lodge?
a) dolphin
b) koala
c) beaver

5 Which mammal has a pouch?
a)   seal
b)   bat
c)   kangaroo

6 Which mammal can fly?
a)   sugar glider
b)   bat
c)   kangaroo

7 Which mammal is the fastest runner?
a)   lion
b)   polar bear
c)   cheetah

8 Which sound does a dolphin make?
a)   whistle
b)   bark
c)   roar

9 Which mammal lives in groups called prides?
a)   dormouse
b)   lion
c)   whale

10 Where does a polar bear live?
a)   desert
b)   Arctic
c)   jungle

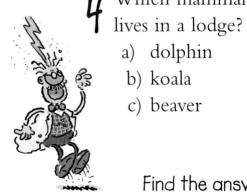

Find the answers on page 160.

Reptiles

Claire Llewellyn

WHAT is a reptile?

Snakes, lizards, tortoises and crocodiles belong to a group of animals called reptiles. Reptiles are all **cold-blooded**, have skeletons, and have tough skins made of plates or scales. Most reptiles lay eggs. Their eggs are always laid on dry land and have either hard or leathery shells.

Snake

Crocodile

HOW many reptiles are there?

There are about 6,500 different kinds of reptile. Scientists have sorted them into four different groups — lizards, snakes, turtles and tortoises, and **crocodilians**. One reptile, the tuatara, does not fit any of these groups. It is a rare, lizard-like creature that is found only in New Zealand.

Tortoise

WHICH reptiles are record-breakers?

Two record-breaking reptiles are the saltwater crocodile and the anaconda snake. A large saltwater crocodile is longer and heavier than two cars parked end to end. An anaconda can grow up to ten metres long and be as heavy as a cow. But some reptiles are tiny – one lizard in the West Indies is no bigger than your thumb!

Lizard

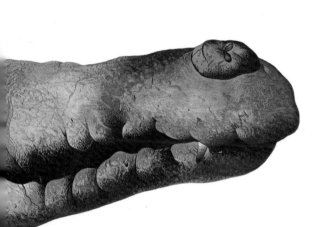

Scientists holding an anaconda

That's Amazing!

There are only 22 kinds of crocodilian, but about 3,800 kinds of lizard!

Some reptiles live very long lives. Giant tortoises can live for 120 years or more!

Now I Know...

★ A reptile is a cold-blooded, scaly animal that has a skeleton.

★ There are about 6,500 different kinds of reptile.

★ Saltwater crocodiles and anacondas are both record-breaking reptiles.

WHICH is the largest lizard?

Look and Find ★ ★ forked tongue

Komodo dragons are enormous lizards that live on some of the islands in Southeast Asia. From snout to tail, they measure about three metres. These lizards are **scavengers**, but they also kill pigs, goats and deer by infecting them with deadly **saliva**. Any animal bitten by a Komodo dragon will die.

That's Amazing!

Some lizards that lose their tail go back later to find it – and eat it!

Some lizards run on their two back legs. The basilisk lizard of South America can even run across water!

Komodo dragons have long claws and short, powerful legs. They can swim, climb trees and run as fast as an athlete at up to 18 kilometres per hour.

Komodo dragons

54

Geckos have no eyelids to keep their eyes clean – they use their tongue to wipe away sand and dirt.

HOW do geckos walk on the ceiling?

Geckos are small, tropical lizards that often live in people's houses. You can see them running up walls and windows, and across the ceiling. They can walk upside down without falling off thanks to ridged pads under their feet. These pads are made up of tiny hooked hairs that help to give the geckos a great grip.

WHY do some lizards lose their tails?

Predators catch some lizards by their tails. The tail is sometimes the only part of a lizard's body that predators can grab. When this happens, a lizard can still escape by breaking off the end of its tail. It is a trick that surprises its predator and gives the lizard time to run away. This lizard's tail (below) looks a little stumpy, but it will soon start to re-grow.

South-eastern five-lined skink losing its tail

Now I Know...

★ The largest lizard is the Komodo dragon.
★ Geckos can walk on the ceiling because of ridged pads under their feet.
★ Some lizards lose their tails to escape from predators.

HOW do crocodiles catch a meal?

Crocodiles catch a meal by stealth. They hide under the water, sealing their eyes, ears, nostrils and throat with special waterproof flaps. When an animal comes to the water to drink, it cannot see or smell the crocodile. Suddenly, the crocodile explodes from the water, grabs the animal, and drowns it.

WHERE would you find a saltie?

'Saltie' is the nickname that Australians give to the saltwater crocodile. Most crocodilians live in freshwater, but salties are found in **estuaries**, swamps along the coast and even far out to sea. A saltie's body is covered with thinner, lighter scales than other crocodilians, and these help it to swim more easily.

Crocodiles can only swallow – not chew – their food. They shake their prey from side to side in their powerful jaws until it breaks into bitesize bits.

Saltwater crocodile attacking

56

WHAT is the difference between alligators and crocodiles?

Alligator

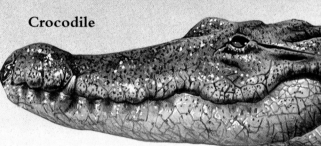
Crocodile

Some crocodilians are hard to tell apart. An alligator's snout is broad and rounded, while a crocodile's is thinner and more pointed. Unlike on an alligator, a large tooth sticks out from a crocodile's jaw when its mouth is shut. Some crocodilians are easier to recognize – gharials have a very slender snout, which is perfect for grabbing fish.

Gharial

That's Amazing!

Crocodilians are always growing new teeth. If any teeth are lost during an attack, new ones grow to take their place!

Male alligators bellow loudly in the breeding season to keep their rivals away!

Wallaby

Now I Know...

★ Crocodiles hide in the water to catch a meal.
★ Salties are found in estuaries, swamps and the sea in Australia.
★ Alligators and crocodiles have different-shaped snouts.

WHAT is the difference between tortoises and turtles?

Tortoises and turtles look very similar, but there are some differences. Tortoises have stumpy feet and live on land. Turtles have flippers, flatter shells, and live in the sea. Both tortoises and turtles have hard, horny beaks. Tortoises feed on juicy plants, while turtles snap up sea creatures. Turtles that live in rivers and streams are called terrapins.

Loggerhead turtle

Mother and baby starred tortoise

HOW fast can a tortoise crawl?

A tortoise's shell is like a suit of armour and makes a heavy load. Because of this, tortoises crawl along slowly at about 0.5 kilometres per hour. Because turtles are lifted up by the salty water of the sea, they do not have to carry their weight. They can swim more than 30 kilometres per hour – as fast as you could cycle!

WHICH terrapin is a crafty fisherman?

When an alligator snapping turtle feels hungry, it lies on the riverbed and opens its beak. On its tongue is a wriggly bit of skin that looks just like a worm. Hungry fish swim up to the 'worm', and are snapped up in the terrapin's sharp beak. These terrapins are named after alligators because they were once thought to be a cross between a terrapin and an alligator.

Alligator snapping turtle fishing

That's Amazing!

Tortoises have lived on earth for at least 200 million years!

Some terrapins have an air tube on the end of their nose, which sticks out like a snorkel!

Every kind of tortoise has its own particular shell pattern. This makes it stand out from other species. It also helps to camouflage the animal, making it harder for predators, such as birds and foxes, to see.

Now I Know...

★ Tortoises have feet and live on land. Turtles have flippers and live in the sea.
★ Tortoises move 0.5 km per hour.
★ The alligator snapping turtle has a clever way of catching fish.

★ Look and Find ★
nostril

WHICH snakes shed their skins?

A snake's skin splits at the snout and peels off like a long, scaly sock. A snake begins to shed its skin by rubbing its snout against a rough surface such as a branch or a stone.

They all do! A snake's skin does not grow with the rest of its body so, as the animal gets bigger, its skin becomes too tight. Every few months, it sheds the top layer of scales. Underneath, it has a brand-new skin in a better-fitting size.

HOW do snakes find their prey?

Snakes use their senses to track down their prey. They have good eyesight, and their flickering, forked tongues pick up smells in the air. Some snakes have an extra sense – tiny holes on the sides of their faces pick up the warmth of animals nearby.

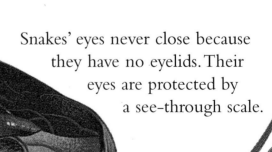

Snakes' eyes never close because they have no eyelids. Their eyes are protected by a see-through scale.

60

Emerald tree boa shedding skin

Brown tree snake shows its fangs

WHY do snakes have fangs?

Some snakes, such as boomslangs and cobras, have a pair of sharp, hollow fangs. Snakes use their fangs to inject poison into their prey. The poison is made in glands inside their cheeks. When a snake attacks, the **venom** is squeezed along a narrow tube and out through the deadly fangs.

That's Amazing!

No snakes are plant-eaters – they all need meat to survive!

We have 29 bones in our backbone – a snake can have up to 400!

Now I Know...

★ All snakes shed their skins several times a year.
★ Snakes have sharp senses to help them find their prey.
★ Some snakes kill by injecting poison through their fangs.

WHERE do turtles lay their eggs?

Female turtles lay their eggs in holes on sandy beaches. Two months later, the eggs **hatch**, and the tiny turtles dig up to the surface and scuttle to the sea. They have to hurry or they will be eaten by seagulls and other predators.

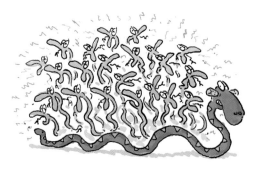

That's Amazing!

Rattlesnakes have about ten babies at a time, but other snakes can have up to 40!

Turtles lay their eggs on moonlit nights. Each turtle lays about 100 eggs before returning to the sea.

WHAT is a snakeling?

A snakeling is a baby snake. Most snakes lay eggs but others, such as boa constrictors and some vipers, are **viviparous** and give birth to live young. As with most other reptiles, the mother does not care for her young. Some snakelings have sharp fangs and venom, and they can take care of themselves!

Snakeling hatching

WHY do crocodiles make good mums?

Female crocodiles guard their nests. When they hear their babies calling, the mums open the nest and help their young to hatch, then gently carry them to the riverbank in their jaws.

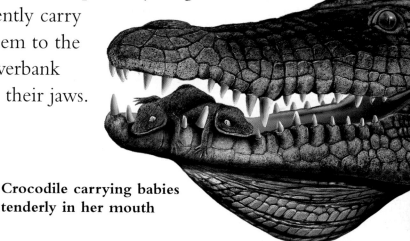

Crocodile carrying babies tenderly in her mouth

Now I Know...

★ Turtles lay their eggs in holes on sandy beaches.
★ A snakeling is a baby snake.
★ Crocodiles, unlike most reptiles, care for their young after they hatch.

WHERE does the leaf-tailed gecko hide?

The leaf-tailed gecko hides on tree branches. It has a ragged shape, flat body, bark-like skin and a tail shaped like a leaf. These features help it to blend in with its background. Camouflage helps animals like the gecko to keep out of sight of predators. But camouflage can help hunters too, by hiding them from their prey!

These leaf-tailed geckos live in the **rainforests** of Australia and Madagascar, an island off the east coast of Africa.

WHY are coral snakes so brightly coloured?

No animal can fail to see the coral snake with its bright red, black and white stripes. The bold colours warn other animals that the snake is venomous and will hurt them if they attack it. The warning keeps predators at bay, and helps coral snakes avoid danger.

Colourful coral snake

64

HOW do chameleons keep out of sight?

Chameleons have a clever way of hiding – their skin colour changes to match their surroundings. When this lizard moves, **cells** in its skin change size, moving grains of colour nearer to the surface or deeper beneath it. It takes about five minutes for a chameleon to change its colour completely.

Green skin is the perfect camouflage for a flap-necked chameleon in the trees.

That's Amazing!

The milk snake has the same colour stripes as the deadly coral snake, but in a different order. Although it is harmless, other animals think it is venomous and keep out of its way!

A chameleon's tongue is as long as its body! And it has a sticky tip to zap flies and other insects!

Now I Know...

★ Leaf-tailed geckos hide on tree branches.
★ Coral snakes are brightly coloured to warn other animals that they are dangerous.
★ Chameleons keep out of sight by changing their skin colour.

Look and Find ★ ★ rattle

HOW does the frilled lizard trick its enemies?

When a frilled lizard is threatened by predators, it raises a flap of skin around its neck, and opens its mouth and hisses. This is just a clever trick. The lizard is quite harmless, but it makes itself look large and fierce to frighten away its enemies!

By raising its flap of skin, a frilled lizard looks about four times larger than it really is.

WHY does a rattlesnake rattle?

If large animals get too near a rattlesnake, it tries to warn them away. It makes a buzzing sound by shaking the dry, scaly rings on the tip of its tail. As soon as animals hear this sound, they move out of harm's way.

Rattlesnake shaking its rattle

Chuckwalla jammed between two rocks

WHICH lizard gets itself into a jam?

The chuckwalla lives in the rocky deserts of North America. When it is frightened, it hides away in cracks in rocks. Then it sucks in air and puffs up its body, jamming itself in so tightly that it cannot be pulled out.

That's Amazing!

The Australian blue-tongued skink scares its enemies by sticking out its extraordinary blue tongue!

The grass snake is a great actor. It puts off its enemies by pretending to be dead!

Now I Know...

★ The frilled lizard tricks its enemies by making itself look fierce.
★ Rattlesnakes rattle their tails to warn away other animals.
★ The chuckwalla squeezes itself between cracks in rocks.

WHY do reptiles live in deserts?

Many animals would find it hard to live in a desert, but reptiles are well-suited to this harsh, dry habitat. Their thick, scaly skin locks in every drop of water and stops them drying out. And, because their energy comes from the sun, they can survive on very little food.

WHAT is the best way of moving over sand?

It can be tricky moving over loose, sandy ground – it is all too easy to sink into the sand instead of moving forwards! The sidewinder rattlesnake has solved this problem by using a movement known as sidewinding. It throws its body into S-shaped loops, and moves them sideways over the ground.

Sidewinder rattlesnake

Desert iguana

Regal horned lizard

Kangaroo rat

HOW does a desert tortoise cool down?

The desert tortoise avoids the hottest part of the day by hiding in an underground burrow. But if, by chance, it is caught in the sun, the tortoise **urinates** on its back two legs. As the urine dries in the desert air, it cools the animal down.

That's Amazing!

The thorny devil from Australia is never thirsty – it drinks the dew that runs off its spines!

A desert tortoise can go more than a year without a drink of water!

Gila monster

Desert tortoises

Now I Know...

★ Reptile bodies are well-adapted to desert life.
★ Moving sideways is a good way of moving over sand.
★ The desert tortoise cools down by urinating on itself.

REPTILES QUIZ

What have you remembered about reptiles? Test what you know and see how much you have learned.

1 What type of reptile is a gharial?
a)   lizard
b)   crocodilian
c)   snake

2 Where do reptiles lay their eggs?
a)   in rivers and lakes
b)   in the sea
c)   on dry land

3 How long can an anaconda grow?
a)   up to ten centimetres
b)   up to two metres
c)   up to ten metres

4 Which reptiles shed their skin?
a) crocodilians
b) tortoises
c) snakes

5 Which reptiles can walk on the ceiling?
a)   snakes
b)   alligators
c)   geckos

6 Which reptile kills with its deadly saliva?
a)   five-lined skink
b)   Komodo dragon
c)   starred tortoise

7 Where do salties live?
a)   in the desert
b)   in rivers and the sea
c)   in the rainforest

8 Which reptile hides in cracks in rocks?
a)   chuckwalla
b)   frilled lizard
c)   desert tortoise

9 How long do turtle eggs take to hatch?
a)   two days
b)   two weeks
c)   two months

10 What part of a rattlesnake rattles?
a)   its tail
b)   its fangs
c)   its tongue

Find the answers on page 160.

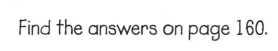

Birds

Angela Wilkes

WHAT is a bird?

Birds are the only animals that have feathers. Most birds can fly and they all have two wings. To help them fly, birds are extremely light. They have **hollow** bones, a covering of feathers and a lightweight beak instead of teeth. Their smooth, **streamlined** shape makes it easy for them to slip through the air. Like us, birds are warm-blooded and breathe air. Unlike us, they lay eggs.

WHY do birds have feathers?

A bird has three different types of feather. Small, fluffy down feathers lie next to the bird's skin and help to keep it warm. Body feathers cover the down feathers and give the bird a streamlined shape. The strong, stiff feathers on a bird's wings and tail are called flight feathers. They slot together tightly to make a smooth surface which helps the bird to fly.

Down feather

Body feathers

Flight feathers

Wing feathers

Tail feathers

A bird's tail helps it to steer and brake when it is flying.

That's Amazing!

A large bird, such as a goose, can have up to 25,000 feathers. Some tiny hummingbirds have fewer than 1,000!

A swan is so light that it is only one quarter of the weight of a dog the same size!

Kingfisher

A bird's beak is made of strong, light horn. Horn is a kind of hard skin.

Birds have scaly legs and feet, with claws at the ends of their toes.

HOW many kinds of bird are there?

There are about 9,000 different species, or kinds, of bird. They come in all shapes and sizes. Some hummingbirds are no larger than a bumblebee, while an ostrich can grow taller than a human. All birds have wings and feathers, even birds which cannot fly, such as the cassowary. Birds are found all over the world. They live in polar areas and in deserts, in hot, steamy rainforests and in back gardens.

Cassowary

The cassowary lives in New Guinea and Australia. It has razor-sharp claws to protect itself against attackers.

Now I Know...

★ Birds are the only animals that have feathers.
★ Feathers are for warmth, streamlining and flying.
★ There are about 9,000 different types of bird.

HOW do birds fly?

Birds usually fly by flapping their wings. A bird has strong chest muscles to pull its wings upwards, then bring them down again. The wing feathers push against the air, which moves the bird forwards and up. Birds twist their wings to turn in the air. Some birds flap their wings fast and others slowly. Some birds rise and dip in the air. Others glide or hover.

A jay jumps into the air and flaps its wings to take off.

Jay

As the bird lifts its wings, the feathers spread apart.

That's Amazing!

Albatrosses run so fast when they take off and land that they need a special runway in their nesting colony!

Swifts only stop flying and land when they are nesting. They even sleep in mid-air!

74

WHY do hummingbirds hover?

Hummingbirds hover so that they can stop in front of flowers and drink the nectar inside. They hold their bodies almost upright and beat their tiny wings backwards and forwards so fast that they make a whirring or humming sound. They are the only birds that can fly sideways, forwards and backwards.

Ruby-throated hummingbird

Then the jay pulls its wings down hard.

WHICH bird is like a glider?

The wandering albatross spends most of its life gliding low above the ocean. It has long, narrow wings and can fly for hours without flapping them. Most seabirds glide. They hold their wings out stiffly and use **currents** of air that rise up from the surface of the sea to keep them in the air and carry them along.

Now I Know...

★ Birds usually fly by flapping their wings up and down.

★ Hummingbirds hover to feed on the nectar inside flowers.

★ An albatross can fly for hours without flapping its wings.

★ Look and Find ★

wasp

WHAT do lorikeets eat?

Birds' beaks are different shapes, depending on what they eat. Lorikeets live in tropical forests where the trees are in flower all year round. The lorikeets feed on the **pollen** and sweet nectar inside the tree flowers. They have short, strong beaks for tearing off flower petals and buds, and brush-tipped tongues for collecting nectar and pollen. They also eat fruit, grasping it firmly in one foot.

Common crossbill

HOW does a crossbill use its beak?

The crossbill has a unique beak, or bill, which crosses over at the tips. The bird uses it just like a tool, to twist apart the scales on pine cones. Then the crossbill hooks out the seeds with its beak or scoops them out with its long tongue. Sometimes it uses its beak to pick bark off a tree trunk, to catch the insects living underneath.

That's Amazing!

Some birds, such as the cattle egret, stand on animals to feed on the insects living in the animal's fur!

A woodpecker's tongue is so long that it can be up to five times the length of its beak!

76

WHY does a woodpecker peck wood?

A woodpecker uses its powerful beak to drill through the bark of a tree in search of grubs. Then it scoops them out with its long, sticky tongue. It also drums its beak loudly against a tree to attract a mate or to warn rival woodpeckers to stay away from its territory.

Rainbow lorikeets

Fig

Eucalyptus buds and flowers

Now I Know...

★ Lorikeets feed on nectar and pollen from tropical tree flowers.
★ A crossbill uses its beak to pick seeds out of pine cones.
★ Woodpeckers drill into wood to find grubs to eat.

WHY do eagles have huge claws?

Eagles are **birds of prey** – they kill other animals to eat. An eagle has very good eyesight. It soars high in the sky, watching the ground below. When the eagle spots prey, it swoops down low and swings its feet forwards. It grabs the prey in its giant, curved claws, called **talons**. The eagle carries the prey back to its nest, where it tears the dead animal apart with its sharp, hooked beak.

WHERE do vultures find their food?

Vultures are scavengers, which means they feed only on dead animals. They circle high in the sky until they see a **carcass**, then flock down to the ground. The vultures peck holes in the carcass and stretch their necks inside. Their heads are bald, which helps to keep them clean as they feed.

An eagle's talons are its main weapon. The forward-pointing toes grab the animal and the back talons kill it.

78

WHEN do owls hunt?

Most owls hunt at night. They eat small animals such as mice and insects. They have big eyes and can see well in dim light, and their hearing is so good they can even find prey in the dark. Owls are silent hunters, because their soft wing feathers muffle any sound when they swoop in for the kill. Usually, owls do not tear up their food before they eat it – they swallow it whole. Later, they cough up balls of fur and bones called **pellets**.

A barn owl with a vole

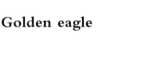

Golden eagle

Rabbit

That's Amazing!

The peregrine falcon can fly faster than any other bird. It dive-bombs its prey at 200 kilometres per hour!

Buzzards can spot prey from as far away as 5 kilometres!

Owls cannot swivel their huge eyes, but they can turn their heads right round to see behind them!

Now I Know...

★ Eagles use their huge claws to catch animals and kill them.
★ Vultures eat dead animals they find on the ground.
★ Owls go hunting for small animals at night.

WHY do peacocks show off?

Before a bird can lay eggs, it has to find a mate. The females usually choose, so male birds do their best to impress them. Peacocks are brightly coloured and have long, shimmering tail feathers. They open these out like fans and rustle them to show off the 'eyes'. The females, called peahens, are a dull brown, so they can nest without enemies noticing them. After the birds have mated, the peahen builds a nest and rears her chicks all on her own.

That's Amazing!

The male frigate bird shows off to females by inflating a huge red pouch below his throat!

Some birds of paradise hang upside down from a branch to impress any females watching!

The peahen pretends to ignore the peacock, but this is all part of finding a mate.

Peahen

WHICH birds dance together?

Japanese cranes dancing

In some species of bird, the males and females look alike. They go through a special **courtship** routine to find a mate. Cranes gather in groups and choose partners by dancing together. They form pairs, then bow, flap their wings, jump into the air and sing duets. Each pair of birds builds a nest, and both birds take part in raising the chicks.

HOW does a bowerbird win a mate?

A male satin bowerbird builds an avenue of twigs, called a bower, to attract females. He uses the bower to display the treasures he has collected. He lays out berries, feathers and shells, all coloured blue like him. He even mashes up berries so he can paint the walls of his bower with blue juice.

Satin bowerbird

Peacock

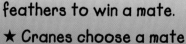

Now I Know...

★ Peacocks show off their beautiful feathers to win a mate.
★ Cranes choose a mate by dancing together.
★ Bowerbirds build courtship bowers to attract females.

WHICH bird weaves its nest?

Birds build nests so that they have a safe, sheltered place to lay their eggs and raise their chicks. Many nests are small and cup-shaped, but some weaver birds in Africa make giant nests by weaving blades of grass together. The male bird weaves a round nest with a long entrance tunnel. He hopes the nest will impress a female enough to mate with him.

A swallow feeding its chicks

The weaver bird starts by making a ring of grass stems. He builds around this to make the rest of the nest.

That's Amazing!

Some weaver birds live in enormous nests that cover a whole treetop. The nests may be 100 years old and have 400 birds living in them!

Gannets and boobies keep their eggs warm by standing on them with their big webbed feet!

WHAT does a swallow use to build its nest?

Swallows build cup-shaped nests out of damp mud and line them with grass or soft feathers. They often build their nests on a ledge or beam inside a barn. Birds build nests out of all kinds of things, from twigs and mosses to silk from spiders' webs.

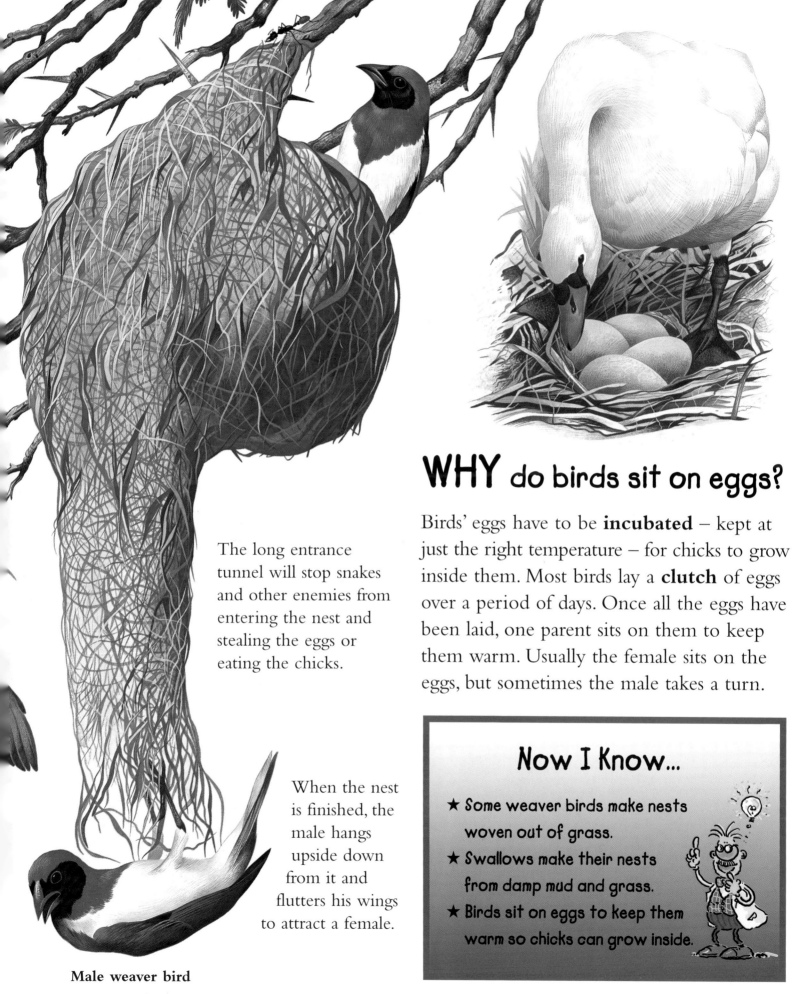

The long entrance tunnel will stop snakes and other enemies from entering the nest and stealing the eggs or eating the chicks.

When the nest is finished, the male hangs upside down from it and flutters his wings to attract a female.

Male weaver bird

WHY do birds sit on eggs?

Birds' eggs have to be **incubated** – kept at just the right temperature – for chicks to grow inside them. Most birds lay a **clutch** of eggs over a period of days. Once all the eggs have been laid, one parent sits on them to keep them warm. Usually the female sits on the eggs, but sometimes the male takes a turn.

Now I Know...

★ Some weaver birds make nests woven out of grass.

★ Swallows make their nests from damp mud and grass.

★ Birds sit on eggs to keep them warm so chicks can grow inside.

Look and Find
feather

WHAT do baby birds eat?

Many baby birds are born naked and blind. They cannot walk or fly, so their parents feed them. Chicks need huge amounts of body-building food, such as insects, because they grow so fast. The parents fly to and fro all day, dropping food into their gaping beaks. The chicks stay in the nest until their feathers have grown and they can fly away. Even then, their parents often carry on helping them to find food.

That's Amazing!

Some cuckoos lay their eggs in other birds' nests. When the cuckoo chick hatches, it pushes the other eggs out of the nest!

A great tit may deliver food to its nest 900 times a day!

The chicks' wide-open beaks are a signal to their parents that they need feeding.

HOW do chicks hatch?

When a chick is ready to hatch, it chips a hole in its eggshell with a sharp point on its beak called an egg tooth. When the hole is big enough, the chick pushes itself out. Ducklings and other birds that nest on the ground have their eyes open when they hatch. They are covered with soft down and can walk immediately.

Ducklings hatching

Grub

An adult blue tit feeding its chicks

WHERE does a shoebill stork raise its chick?

Shoebill storks live on African marshes among tall, thick reeds. They build nests on floating beds of plants and usually have one chick. To feed it, they cough up fish and water snakes that they have already eaten. During the heat of the day, the mother shades her chick from the sun and sprinkles big beakfuls of water over it to keep it cool.

Now I Know...

★ Baby birds eat lots of insects and other body-building food.
★ To hatch, a chick pecks a hole in its shell with its egg tooth.
★ A shoebill stork raises its chick on a floating bed of plants.

85

WHERE do geese fly in autumn?

Brent geese spend the summer in the far north, where their chicks hatch. But winter in the north is very cold and food is hard to find, so in autumn, the geese fly south. They fly thousands of kilometres to warmer places where there is plenty of food. The next spring, they return to their summer home. These journeys are called **migrations**. Many birds migrate. Some fly all the way without stopping. Others land from time to time, to rest and feed before carrying on their way.

Brent geese

Geese migrate in large flocks. They usually fly in a V-shaped group and take it in turns to be leader, so none of them becomes too tired.

That's Amazing!

Bar-headed geese fly across the highest mountains in the world to reach their winter homes. They fly nearly as high in the sky as jet planes!

Snow geese can fly nearly 3,000 kilometres in just two days!

86

WHICH bird makes the longest journey?

Arctic terns fly right across the world and back every year. In late summer, they leave the countries around the Arctic Ocean and fly to Antarctica, where summer is just beginning. In spring, they fly back again. This round trip of 25,000 kilometres means they can enjoy summer all year round.

Arctic tern

Geese honk to each other as they fly, to keep in touch with all the other members of the group.

HOW do migrating birds find their way?

Migrating birds follow the same routes every year. They may use the position of the sun and the stars to help them find their way. Also, birds often follow familiar features in the landscape below them. They fly along mountain chains, river valleys and coastlines.

Now I Know...

★ Brent geese fly south in autumn, to find food in a warmer place.
★ Arctic terns travel the furthest when they migrate.
★ Birds may use the sun and stars to help find their way.

★ Look and Find ★ snake

HOW do macaws recognize each other?

Birds communicate with each other by sight, as well as by sound. Macaws are colourful parrots that live in groups in tropical rainforests. Each type of macaw has its own bright colours and markings, rather like a uniform. The birds recognize each other by the colours and patterns of their feathers, so they know to which group they belong. Other birds may not be brightly coloured, but they have markings on their faces or bodies to help them recognize each other.

WHICH bird changes colour?

Many birds use colour to hide from enemies. This is called camouflage. All birds moult, but the ptarmigan moults twice a year, changing colour to suit the season. In winter, when snow is on the ground, it has white feathers. In spring, it moults and grows brown feathers that blend in with the heaths where it lives. When winter comes, it moults again and grows white feathers.

That's Amazing!

A bittern's booming call can be heard for five kilometres across the reed beds where it lives!

The twit-twoo call of a tawny owl is actually made by two birds. One owl calls 'twit' and the other replies 'twoo'!

Scarlet macaws

Macaws often gather on river banks to eat clay. This helps them to **digest** the tough seeds that they eat.

WHY do birds sing?

Many birds, such as the robin, sing to send messages to other birds. Each type of songbird has its own song. By singing, birds show who they are and claim a patch of their own. In spring, many birds sing together loudly at daybreak. The sound they make is known as the dawn chorus.

Now I Know...

★ Macaws recognize each other by the colours of their feathers.
★ Moulting allows a ptarmigan to change colour twice a year.
★ Birds sing to announce who they are to other birds.

BIRDS QUIZ

What have you remembered about birds? Test what you know and see how much you have learned.

1 What do hummingbirds like to eat?
a) seeds
b) fruit
c) nectar

2 Which bird has a long, sticky tongue?
a) macaw
b) woodpecker
c) cassowary

3 Which bird feeds on animal carcasses?
a) eagle
b) owl
c) vulture

4 Which bird can change colour?
a) robin
b) ptarmigan
c) eagle

5 What is the pattern on a peacock's feathers?
a) eyes
b) ears
c) nose

6 What is a swallow's nest made out of?
a) stones
b) leaves
c) mud

7 Which bird makes the longest journey?
a) Arctic tern
b) jay
c) vulture

8 Which feathers keep a bird warm?
a) flight feathers
b) down feathers
c) body feathers

9 Where does a shoebill stork build its nest?
a) on a river bank
b) on floating plants
c) on a chimney top

10 How does an albatross usually fly?
a) it hovers
b) it glides
c) it flaps its wings fast

Find the answers on page 160.

Fish and Sharks

Stephen Savage

Look and Find
★ ★
stonefish

WHAT is a fish?

A fish is an animal that lives in water, has a body covered in scales and fins to help it swim. Most types of fish have a bony skeleton and an air-filled **swim bladder** that helps them to float, even when they stop swimming. Fish are cold-blooded, although a few fast-swimming fish have bodies that are slightly warmer than the surrounding water.

HOW many types of fish are there?

There are about 28,000 different types of fish. They live in the salty oceans and seas all around the globe, and in the world's rivers, lakes and ponds. Fish can be very different in shape, size and colour, for example the tall batfish or the long-bodied flutemouth. The largest fish, at up to 18 metres long, is the whale shark. The smallest is a type of goby which is just one centimetre long.

That's Amazing!

Hagfish are primitive fish with no fins or jaws. They produce huge amounts of slime and even tie themselves in knots.

Grouper

Flutemouth

Moray eel

Humbug

Butterfly fish

92

Battish

Clown fish

Moorish idol

Spotted triggerfish

Boxfish

Fish bodies are covered in slimy scales.

WHY are fish slimy?

Fish feel slippery because their bodies are covered in slime. These slimy coats are produced by the skin, and protect the fish against disease and some **parasites**. The slime covers wounds and scratches, preventing infection. It may also help the fish slip through the water more easily. Some types of fish have poisonous slime to protect them from predators.

Now I know...

★ A fish is an animal that lives in water. It has a skeleton, scales and fins.

★ There are about 28,000 different types of fish.

★ Fish produce a protective slime that coats their skin.

93

Look and Find
gill cover

HOW do fish breathe?

Fish breathe water, unlike land animals, which breathe air. Inside a fish's head is a pair of delicate **gills**, each protected by a gill cover. The fish draws water in through its mouth. The water passes over the gills and out through the gill cover slit. The gills take up **oxygen** from the water.

That's Amazing!

Lungfish can breathe air. If their lake dries up, they burrow into the mud and live in a special mucus cocoon.

94

DO all fish have gills?

All fish have gills, but some, like the bichir, also have an extra method of breathing. The bichir fish lives in rivers and lakes in Africa. It has gills, but it also uses its swim bladder like a lung. The bichir breathes by gulping air at the surface of the water. This means it can live in water where there is very little oxygen, such as in slow-moving rivers.

Mouth

WHAT are spiracles?

Rays are flat-bodied fish that often rest on the seabed. Their mouths are on the underside of their heads, which means they are no use for breathing. Behind each eye is a special hole called a spiracle. These pump water over the gills, so the rays can breathe even when they're resting on the sand.

This resting perch is motionless except for small movements of the mouth and gill covers.

Now I know...

★ Fish breathe in water through their gills. They get oxygen from the water.

★ All fish have gills, but some can breathe air as well.

★ Spiracles are holes which pump water over the gills.

HOW do fish swim?

Most fish swim in an S-shaped motion, using side-to-side movements. A fish's tail pushes it forwards while the fins on the top and bottom of its body keep it upright. Fins on the side of the body can be used as brakes. Some fish can remain still in the water, using their fins to keep their position.

WHAT are flying fish?

Flying fish live near the surface of the water in warm seas. They have an unusual way of escaping danger. Their two large fins look like wings. When attacked, flying fish can leap out of the water and glide for a distance of ten metres or more.

Flying fish

96

Koi carp use their fins to keep their place in the water

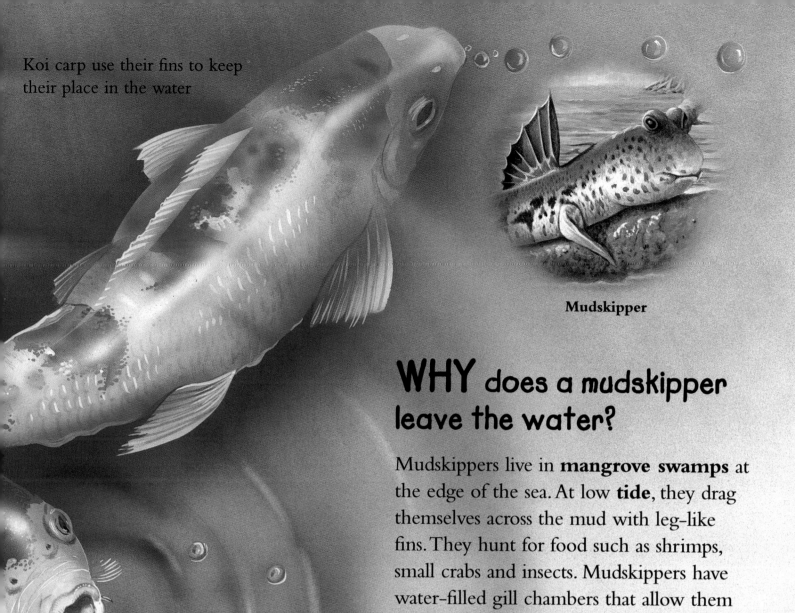

Mudskipper

WHY does a mudskipper leave the water?

Mudskippers live in **mangrove swamps** at the edge of the sea. At low **tide**, they drag themselves across the mud with leg-like fins. They hunt for food such as shrimps, small crabs and insects. Mudskippers have water-filled gill chambers that allow them to breathe out of water. They spend about three-quarters of their time out of water.

That's Amazing!

Climbing perch live in water but can travel over land using their tail and fins. They can breathe air and some types stay out of water for several days.

The sailfish is the fastest swimmer, at 70 km per hour.

Now I know...

★ Fish swim in an S-shaped movement, which pushes them forwards through the water.
★ Flying fish can 'glide' in the air for ten metres.
★ Mudskippers can 'walk' across the mud at low tide.

97

WHY do fish live in shoals?

★ Look and Find ★ sergeant fish

In the open sea there are many dangers. Fish often live in a group called a **shoal** for safety – sometimes hundreds of the same type of fish congregate together. This means they have a better chance of spotting danger and each individual fish has a better chance of escaping if the shoal is attacked. In a shoal, the striped bodies of the sergeant fish become a mass of stripes, making it difficult for a predator to pick out one fish to attack.

Shoal of sergeant fish

HOW does the lionfish hunt?

The beautiful lionfish often lives on **coral reefs**, where it hunts small fish and shrimps. It uses the elaborate fins on the side of its head to herd prey. Once the prey has been cornered, the lionfish opens its mouth quickly and sucks the animal inside. The lionfish has nothing to fear from predators. Its brightly coloured body is a warning that the spines on its back are poisonous.

Lionfish trap prey in their gills.

Flatfish, such as this plaice, hide on the seabed.

WHY do flatfish change colour?

Many types of fish have bodies coloured so they can blend in with the surrounding habitat. This is called camouflage. Flatfish can actually change the colour of their body to match the seabed. This not only helps them avoid predators, but also helps them catch food. Small fish, crabs and shrimps do not notice the flatfish until it is too late.

That's Amazing!

Puffer fish inflate their bodies, making them too big to eat.

Piranhas live in shoals and can eat large mammals!

Now I know...

★ Many fish live in large groups, called shoals, for safety.
★ The lionfish hunts by herding prey using its delicate fins.
★ Flatfish hide from predators and prey by changing colour to blend in with the seabed.

HOW do fish breed?

Most types of fish lay hundreds or even thousands of tiny eggs. These are scattered on the seabed or riverbed and many will be eaten by other fish. Most fish do not look after their young – once the eggs are laid, the job is done. Some, though, make a huge effort to find the best place to lay their eggs. Salmon spend their adult lives at sea. When it is time for them to **spawn**, they make a long journey back to the river where they hatched.

WHICH fish make a bubble nest?

Siamese fighting fish

Siamese fighting fish, which live in the slow-moving rivers of southeast Asia, protect their eggs from predators. The male builds a nest of air bubbles, coated in **mucus** from its mouth to stop them bursting. He collects the eggs and blows them into the nest, which he then guards.

WHICH male fish has babies?

The females of some types of fish give birth to live young. These hatch from eggs kept inside the female's body. Seahorses are unusual because it is the male who actually gives birth. The female seahorse lays her eggs in a special brood pouch on the body of the male seahorse. The eggs become attached to the wall inside the pouch and are **nourished** until they are ready to hatch. The baby seahorses all leave the pouch at the same time.

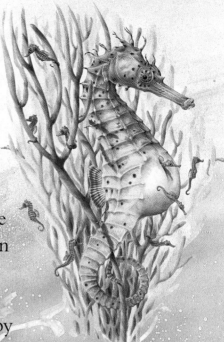

Male seahorse and young

That's Amazing!

Mouthbrooder fish carry their eggs, and later their young, in their mouths.

The bitterling fish deposits its eggs inside a freshwater mussel for safety.

Salmon can leap up small waterfalls to reach the river where they will spawn.

Now I know...

★ Fish breed by laying eggs, often hundreds or thousands of them.
★ Some fish, like the Siamese fighting fish, protect their eggs from predators.
★ Seahorses hatch from eggs nourished in the male's body.

Look and Find
★ ★
shrimp

WHICH fish live with other animals?

Some fish live with other sea creatures, in a partnership where both animals benefit. This is called **symbiosis**. Large sea anemones, which are found on coral reefs, catch food with their poisonous, stinging tentacles. Clown fish can live among the tentacles without being stung. Other fish trying to catch the clown fish may be stung and eaten by the anemone. In return, the clown fish helps protect the anemone from harmful creatures.

That's Amazing!

Remora fish cling to any large moving object, such as whales, sharks, ships and even divers!

The pearl fish lives inside the body of a sea cucumber.

HOW does the cleaner wrasse clean?

The tiny cleaner wrasse lives on coral reefs, where it provides a cleaning service for bigger fish such as the coral hind. The cleaner wrasse performs a special dance to show it is ready to clean. The coral hind keeps still while the cleaner wrasse eats parasites and dead skin from its body, mouth and gills. The coral hind gets a clean, and the wrasse gets a meal.

102

WHICH fish lives with a shrimp?

The seabed is a dangerous place for shrimps and small fish. The Luther's goby has teamed up with a shrimp that is almost blind. The shrimp uses its claws to dig a burrow where both can shelter from danger. When they leave the burrow to search for food, they stay together. The goby alerts the shrimp to any danger so that both can hide.

Luther's goby with its partner shrimp

Clown fish live safely among the poisonous tentacles of sea anemones.

Now I know...

★ Some fish have partnerships with other animals which are useful to both creatures.
★ Tiny cleaner fish feed inside the mouths of bigger fish.
★ Luther's goby lives in a burrow made by a shrimp.

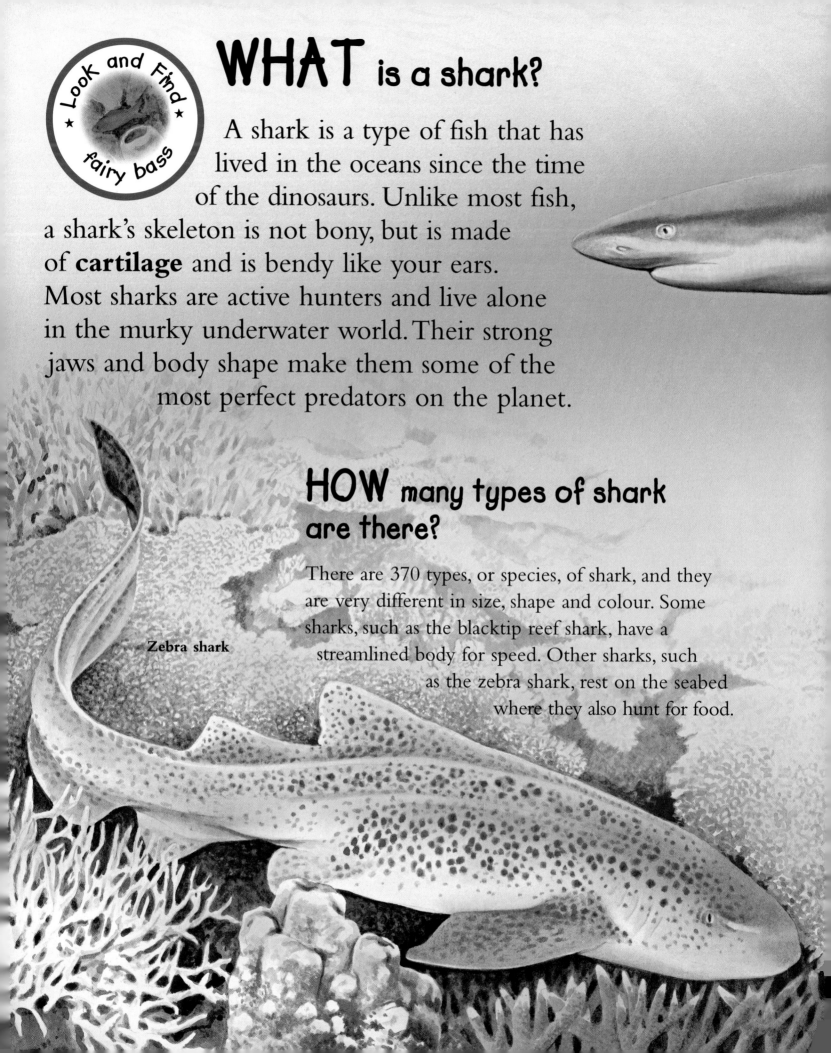

WHAT is a shark?

A shark is a type of fish that has lived in the oceans since the time of the dinosaurs. Unlike most fish, a shark's skeleton is not bony, but is made of **cartilage** and is bendy like your ears. Most sharks are active hunters and live alone in the murky underwater world. Their strong jaws and body shape make them some of the most perfect predators on the planet.

HOW many types of shark are there?

There are 370 types, or species, of shark, and they are very different in size, shape and colour. Some sharks, such as the blacktip reef shark, have a streamlined body for speed. Other sharks, such as the zebra shark, rest on the seabed where they also hunt for food.

Zebra shark

Blacktip reef shark

WHICH other fish are a type of shark?

Ray fish have a skeleton made of cartilage, so they are a type of shark. They have flat bodies with wing-like fins and appear to 'fly' through the water. Most rays have their mouth on the underside of their head for eating animals living on the seabed.

That's Amazing!

Ancient relatives of sharks lived in the oceans 400 million years ago!

Many small animals survive because sharks hunt the creatures that eat them!

Blue-spot ray

Now I Know...

★ A shark is a type of fish with a skeleton made of cartilage.
★ There are 370 types of shark, which vary in size and shape.
★ Ray fish are a type of shark that have wing-like fins.

105

Look and Find ★ ★
gill slits

HOW can a shark drown?

Sharks breathe by taking in oxygen from the water through their gills. Large sharks can breathe *only* when water flows past their gills. This means they have to keep swimming, or they will stop breathing and drown. The smaller, bottom-living sharks also breathe by pumping water over their gills, so they are able to rest on the seabed.

WHAT helps a great white shark to keep swimming?

Many large sharks swim with side-to-side movements of their tails, followed by a long graceful glide to save energy. Unlike most sharks, a great white has a body temperature that is higher than the surrounding sea. This allows its swimming muscles to work better, so it can swim faster for longer.

WHICH shark is the greatest traveller?

Scientists have been able to find out which sharks travel the furthest. They attach small **tags** to the sharks and then record where they turn up. The blue shark holds the record for the longest distance travelled. Blue sharks often swim 2,000 to 3,000 kilometres to mate or search for food. Scientists have also found that bottom-living sharks often stay close to the area where they were born.

That's Amazing!

When leaping out of water, a mako shark can move at 35 km per hour!

A record-holding blue shark travelled 5,980 km from Brazil to New York!

Blue sharks normally swim alone, but several may appear together when there is a shoal of squid in one place.

Now I Know...

★ Large sharks stop breathing and drown if they stop swimming.

★ A great white shark's high body temperature helps it swim faster for longer.

★ The blue shark is the greatest traveller.

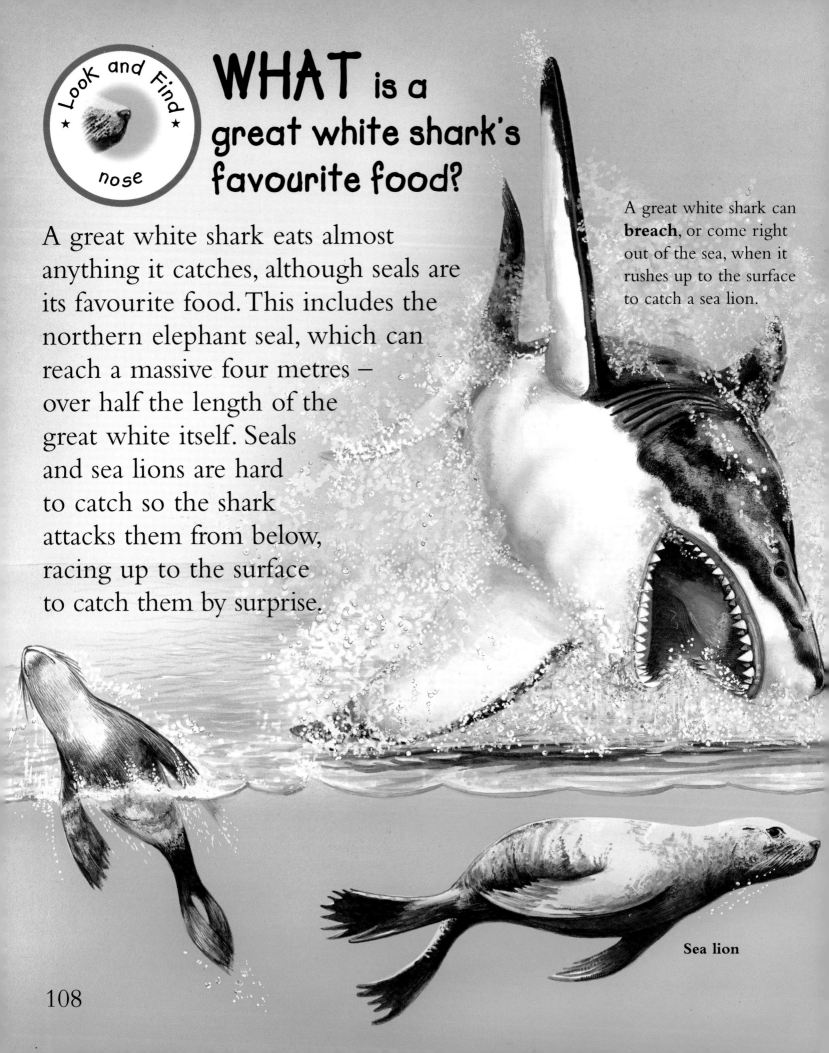

Look and Find
★ ★
nose

WHAT is a great white shark's favourite food?

A great white shark eats almost anything it catches, although seals are its favourite food. This includes the northern elephant seal, which can reach a massive four metres – over half the length of the great white itself. Seals and sea lions are hard to catch so the shark attacks them from below, racing up to the surface to catch them by surprise.

A great white shark can **breach**, or come right out of the sea, when it rushes up to the surface to catch a sea lion.

Sea lion

That's Amazing!

An adult basking shark can filter 9,000 litres of seawater an hour!

Large sharks often swallow strange objects such as bottles, car number plates, cans and coats!

WHICH shark has the most varied diet?

The tiger shark has the most varied diet of any shark. It eats many different types of fish, and even eats seabirds as they rest on the surface of the sea. A tiger shark's razor-sharp teeth can cut through the tough shells of sea turtles and horseshoe crabs. Young tiger sharks even eat very poisonous sea snakes.

HOW does a basking shark eat plankton?

The basking shark swims through the sea with its mouth wide open. Seawater enters its mouth, then passes out through its gills. Special bristles attached to the inside of their gills trap or **filter** out plankton from the water.

Basking shark swimming with its mouth open to catch plankton

Now I Know...

★ Seals are a great white shark's favourite food.
★ Tiger sharks eat many different fish and animals.
★ Basking sharks filter plankton from seawater.

HOW are lemon sharks born?

A female lemon shark gives birth to young called pups, which have grown inside her for several months. She swims into shallow water and usually gives birth to between four and ten pups, one at a time. After resting on the seabed for a short while, each pup will swim off, breaking the cord that joins it to its mother. The pups then have to look after themselves!

That's Amazing!

A whale shark can give birth to as many as 300 pups!

While still in its mother's body, a baby grey nurse shark will attack and eat its unborn brothers and sisters!

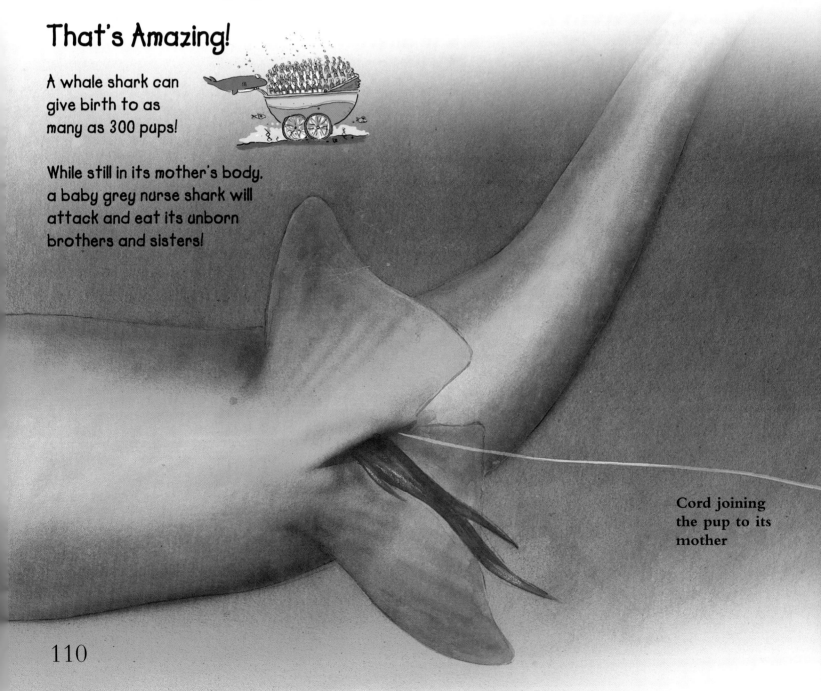

Cord joining the pup to its mother

WHICH sharks lay eggs?

Some small sharks, such as dogfish, cat sharks, carpet sharks and horn sharks, lay 20 to 25 eggs at a time. Each egg is protected within a special egg case, which is either attached to seaweed or hidden on the seabed. The baby shark will grow inside the egg case. The shark feeds from the **yolk sac** attached to its body. It will hatch after several months.

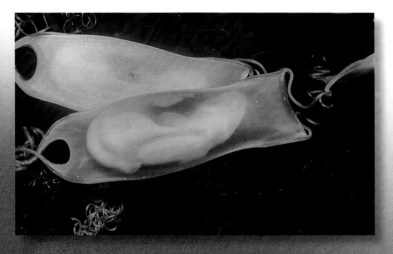

Dogfish attached to yolk sac in an egg case

WHY do sharks have so few pups?

Many fish lay thousands of eggs, but most of the fish that hatch do not survive because they are eaten by other fish. However, most sharks only need to produce a few eggs. These develop inside the mother or in an egg case. When sharks are born or hatch, they are much bigger than many other fish, so most avoid being eaten.

Hammerhead shark pups

Now I Know...

★ Baby lemon shark pups develop inside their mother.
★ Some small sharks lay eggs protected by egg cases.
★ Sharks produce large young that can avoid being eaten.

Lemon shark pup swimming away from its mother

FISH AND SHARKS QUIZ

What have you remembered about fish and sharks? Test what you know and see how much you have learned.

1 What do fish use for breathing?
a) tail
b) scales
c) gills

2 Which is the largest type of fish?
a) whale shark
b) Luther's goby
c) salmon

3 Where do mudskippers live?
a) mangrove swamps
b) Arctic waters
c) fast-flowing streams

4 Which male fish has babies?
a) angel fish
b) carp
c) seahorse

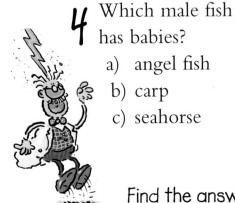

5 Which fish lives with a sea anemone?
a) clown fish
b) sergeant fish
c) pearl fish

6 Why do scientists tag sharks?
a) to reduce shark attacks
b) track distances travelled
c) to measure them

7 Which shark can have 300 young?
a) blue shark
b) whale shark
c) lemon shark

8 Where do zebra sharks hunt for food?
a) in rivers
b) in the deep ocean
c) on the seabed

9 Which shark travels the furthest?
a) lemon shark
b) great white shark
c) blue shark

10 What does a basking shark eat?
a) sea turtles
b) flatfish
c) plankton

Find the answers on page 160.

Seashore

Angela Wilkes

WHAT is a seashore?

All the land on earth – every island and continent – has sea all around it. Where the land meets the sea, there is a seashore. And a seashore is not like other places because parts of it are underwater for some of the day, and uncovered at other times. Seashores provide a home for all kinds of interesting plants and animals.

Red-tailed tropic bird flying out to sea to fish

Green turtles come ashore to lay their eggs in the sand every two to four years.

That's Amazing!

Sea covers two-thirds of earth's surface!

Around the Arctic and Antarctic the seashores are covered in snow and ice!

HOW are seashores different around the world?

Seashores are different depending on whether they are in a warm or cold place, how windy it is and what type of rocks form the land. Some seashores are just rocky ledges or tall cliffs. Some are tropical mangrove swamps. Others have beaches fringed with coral reefs. Beaches can also be sandy or covered in pebbles. Icy seashores are home to only a few animals such as penguins, but many different animals can live on warmer shores.

Rock pools are found on rocky shores. They are home to many different animals such as crabs.

WHERE can you find animals on the seashore?

Most seashore animals hide away in sheltered places. Molluscs and worms live on rocks or under the sand. Fish swim in the sea. Birds search for food along the shore and build their nests on cliffs. Sand dunes make a dry home for reptiles and insects.

Now I know...

★ A seashore is where the land meets the sea.
★ There are many different kinds of seashore around the world.
★ Animals on the seashore shelter in places where they can hide.

115

WHY do kittiwakes nest on cliffs?

Tall cliffs and rocky islands make safe nesting places for kittiwakes and other seabirds. Here, they are close to the sea and the fish they eat. But they are safely out of the reach of enemies, such as rats and foxes. Kittiwakes crowd on rocky ledges to build their nests of seaweed and mud. Other birds build nests with sticks, or lay their eggs straight on the rocks.

That's Amazing!

Guillemots lay eggs on cliff ledges only a few centimetres wide!

American bald eagles build the biggest bird nests!

HOW do herring gull chicks feed?

Herring gulls catch fish, molluscs and crabs to eat. When a parent gull returns to the nest, the chick taps the red spot on its parent's beak. This makes the parent cough up the mushy food it has just eaten to feed the chick.

Herring gull feeding chick

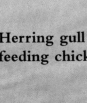

Look and Find ★ ★ cormorant

116

WHERE do puffins lay their eggs?

Puffins nest on cliff tops in spring and summer. They dig holes in the soft **turf** with their large, stripy beaks. Or they lay their eggs in old rabbit burrows, where they will be safely tucked away. Puffins often stand guard near their burrows. When their eggs have hatched and the chicks have grown, the puffins fly out to sea for the winter.

Herring gull

Puffin

Gannets

Kittiwakes

Now I know...

★ Seabirds nest on cliffs where they are safe from enemies.
★ Herring gulls cough up food for their chicks to eat.
★ Puffins lay their eggs in burrows on the cliff tops.

Look and Find
★ ★
sea pea

WHAT are sand dunes?

On wide, sandy beaches, strong winds often blow dry sand about. Sometimes the sand is blown towards tough grasses at the back of the beach. Then it can build up into hills called dunes. The grasses that grow on the dunes hold the sand in place with their spreading roots. As more sand piles up, the dunes grow bigger. A thin layer of soil builds up, so more plants grow. These attract many kinds of special animals.

Clouded yellow butterfly

Yellow horned-poppy

Grasshopper

HOW do plants survive on sand dunes?

Plants on sand dunes have to be tough, because the salt breezes and sun can be strong, and there is very little water. Most plants grow close to the ground and have long, spreading roots that hold them firmly in place. Many plants have fat, waxy leaves that will not dry out, or hairy leaves that trap tiny drops of water.

Greater bird's-foot trefoil

118

WHICH animals live there?

The grasses and flowers on dunes attract insects such as grasshoppers and butterflies. Lizards scuttle across the warm sand. Birds feed on insects in the daytime. Rabbits, toads, snails and mice come out to feed at night. Foxes begin hunting for prey in the evening when it is cooler. The tracks and trails of many animals can be seen across the dunes in the early morning.

Foxes and their cubs visit sand dunes in the evening to hunt for prey such as rabbits, insects and mice.

That's Amazing!

Marram grass grows faster if it is covered by sand!

If there were no plants to hold the sand in place, dunes would constantly move and change shape!

Butterflies are attracted to the sand dunes by the colourful flowers on which they feed.

Dark green fritillary butterfly

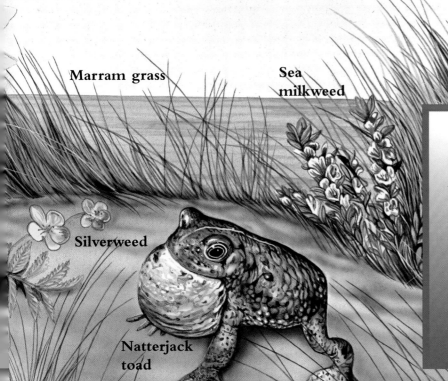

Marram grass

Sea milkweed

Silverweed

Natterjack toad

Now I know...

★ Dunes are hills of sand that form at the back of some beaches.
★ Dune plants have long roots and leaves that do not dry out.
★ Insects, lizards, toads, rabbits and foxes live on sand dunes.

HOW do jellyfish get stranded?

Look and Find ★ ★ cockle shell

Along the seashore the tide comes in twice a day, then goes out again. At every high tide, seaweed and other objects are washed up onto the shore, then left behind as the sea goes out at low tide. A long wiggly line of seaweed and debris across a beach shows where the high tide line is. During storms, when the sea is rough, jellyfish are sometimes thrown ashore at high tide and left **stranded**.

That's Amazing!

Huge seeds of the coco-de-mer palm drift for thousands of kilometres!

The highest tides are at the Bay of Fundy in Canada. They can rise over 14 m (the height of a five-storey building)!

Herring gulls

Bladder wrack

120

WHERE do shells come from?

Shells once had small animals called molluscs living inside them. The hard shells protected their soft bodies. Some shells, such as whelks, are in one piece and some have coils. Others, such as mussels, have two halves joined together by a tiny hinge.

WHAT can you find on the high tide line?

On the beach there will be seaweeds, seashells, interesting bits of **driftwood**, sandhoppers, dead crabs and starfish. You may also find mermaid's purses (the egg cases of sharks and rays), and the skeletons of fish and birds. Be careful not to touch any stranded jellyfish, as they can sting you.

Common starfish

Stranded jellyfish

Mermaid's purse

Whelks

Sandhopper

Now I know...

★ Sea creatures are sometimes stranded on the seashore at high tide.
★ Shells once had molluscs living inside them.
★ You can find many different things along the high tide line.

Look and Find limpet

WHY do lugworms live under the sand?

It is always cool and wet under the sand, so it makes a good hiding-place for animals that dig burrows. Molluscs, lugworms and many other creatures live in burrows under the sand. There, they are hidden from predators such as birds and crabs. The wet sand also keeps them from drying out in the wind and sun.

HOW do burrowers feed?

Molluscs come up to feed when the tide is in. They stick tiny feeding tubes out of their shells and suck up seawater. They filter out bits of food then pump out the water. Lugworms swallow sand as they burrow, eating any food they find. They squirt out the waste sand behind them, forming worm casts.

Worm cast

Sand dollar

Cockle

Pen shell

Lugworm

122

WHERE do purple sea urchins dig their burrows?

Purple sea urchins dig their burrows in solid rock. They gnaw at the rock with their mouths and wiggle their tough spines around to scrape out a channel. They often get stuck in their burrows as they grow larger.

That's Amazing!

Razor shells can dig half of their shell into the sand in just one second!

A Californian sea urchin took 20 years to drill into a solid steel girder!

Piddock

Tellin

Razor shell

Now I know...

★ Lugworms and molluscs burrow under the sand to hide.
★ Burrowers have feeding tubes that filter food from seawater.
★ Purple sea urchins dig into rocks with their mouths and spines.

HOW do oystercatchers catch their food?

Look and Find ★ ★ anemone

As the tide goes out, wading birds move along the shore looking for food. Oystercatchers like to eat worms, and molluscs such as mussels. They use their sharp orange beaks to lever the molluscs off the rocks, and some hammer the shells with their beaks until the shells smash. Others use their beaks to pull the shells apart and reach the juicy flesh inside.

Turnstones flick pebbles over, looking for the shrimps and molluscs hiding underneath.

Oystercatcher

That's Amazing!

Godwits have super-sensitive beaks that can feel creepy crawlies moving in the sand or mud below them!

Plovers pretend to be hurt if their eggs or chicks are in danger, to lure enemies away from their nest!

WHY do curlews have such long beaks?

Wading birds have beaks that are just the right shape for poking into soft sand or mud to look for food. A curlew has a specially long beak to probe deep down into the sand to feel for worms and molluscs. Plovers and other birds with short beaks look for food near the surface of the sand or in the water. This means different birds can feed together, but do not compete for the same food.

WHERE do plovers lay their eggs?

Plovers live on pebbly beaches and lay their eggs in shallow hollows on the ground. Their eggs are pale and speckled like the stones around them, so they are well camouflaged. The mother bird's feathers also match her surroundings, so that enemies do not spot her as she sits on her eggs.

Curlew

Black-headed gull

Now I know...

★ An oystercatcher can open shells with its sharp beak.
★ A curlew's long beak helps it search for food in the sand.
★ A plover lays its camouflaged eggs in shallow hollows on pebbly beaches.

WHAT lives in a rock pool?

Beneath the calm surface of a rock pool there is a busy underwater world. Seaweeds grow there, and all kinds of animals can hide and feed safely underwater when the tide is out. Shellfish and anemones cling to the rocks, crabs scuttle across the sand, and small fish swim to and fro.

A starfish wraps its arms around a shell and pulls it open so it can eat the animal inside.

1 Beadlet anemone
2 Common starfish
3 Blenny
4 Limpet
5 Hermit crab
6 Sea slug
7 Common sea urchin
8 Mussels

126

WHY do limpets cling to rocks?

Molluscs have to be able to hold tightly onto rocks or they would be smashed by strong waves. A limpet seals itself onto rocks with a strong muscular foot, but can still move around. Mussels are attached to rocks by **byssus threads**. A barnacle cements itself to a rock and stays there all its life.

HOW do sea urchins eat?

Spiny sea urchins move across rocks by gripping on with thin tube feet that are like suckers. Their mouths are right underneath their bodies. Sea urchins graze on seaweeds and tiny plants. They eat by scraping plants off the rocks with their five powerful teeth.

That's Amazing!

Barnacles attract food by waving their feathery legs about!

Some sea urchins use pebbles, shells and seaweeds to disguise themselves!

Now I know...

★ A rock pool is a hiding place for many different sea animals.
★ Limpets cling onto rocks for safety.
★ Sea urchins eat using their powerful hidden teeth.

127

WHY do crabs have claws?

Look and Find
whelk

Crabs use their claws to pick up food and tear it apart. They also use them as weapons to fight off attackers. Male crabs have larger claws than female crabs. Most crabs have tough shells like armour, to protect them from enemies. Even so, they are often eaten by shore birds, octopuses, and mammals such as seals and otters.

This crab has its claws up, ready to defend itself from attackers.

HOW do shrimps and prawns swim?

Shrimps and prawns swim over the seabed using the feathery legs on the back halves of their bodies like paddles. They can swim backwards by flicking their fan-shaped tails beneath them. As they swim, they pick up any bits of food they find using the claws on their two front legs.

Common prawns

WHERE do lobsters find their food?

Lobsters find their food in shallow water near the seashore. They usually hide during the day and come out to feed at night. They are scavengers, eating dead or dying fish and animals. Most lobsters live near one seashore all their lives. But some lobsters migrate to other seashores, probably to find a new place to feed.

Norway lobster

That's Amazing!

Each year, thousands of spiny lobsters migrate over 100 km in single file along the seabed near the coast of Florida, USA!

Hermit crabs do not have shells of their own, but move into empty seashells!

HOME SWEET HOME

Now I know...

★ Crabs use their claws to eat and to fight off attackers.

★ Shrimps and prawns swim using their back legs and tail.

★ Lobsters are scavengers that find food in shallow water.

Common shrimp

SEASHORE QUIZ

What have you remembered about the seashore? Test what you know and see how much you have learned.

1 How often does the tide go in and out?
a)   once a week
b)   once a day
c)   twice a day

2 Where do kittiwakes build their nests?
a)   on cliff tops
b)   on rocky ledges
c)   on sand dunes

3 Which plants hold sand dunes in place?
a)   seaweeds
b)   grasses
c)   poppies

4 What is a mermaid's purse?
a) an egg case
b) a shell
c) a plant

5 Which animal burrows into rocks?
a)   purple sea urchin
b)   lugworm
c)   cockle

6 Which shellfish stays in one place for life?
a)   limpet
b)   tellin
c)   barnacle

7 Which animals can swim backwards?
a)   crabs
b)   shrimps and prawns
c)   jellyfish

8 Which birds sometimes nest in old rabbit burrows?
a)   puffins
b)   gannets
c)   herring gulls

9 What marks the high tide line?
a)   rocks
b)   grass
c)   seaweed

10 Which bird has a long, curved beak?
a)   oystercatcher
b)   curlew
c)   plover

Find the answers on page 160.

Rainforest

Angela Wilkes

WHAT is a rainforest?

A rainforest is a dense, steamy forest that grows in tropical countries where it is hot all the time. Millions of giant trees grow close together, draped in exotic plants and trailing **creepers**. It pours with rain nearly every day and there are no seasons, so the trees stay green all year round. More types of plants and animals live in rainforests than anywhere else.

Gibbon

WHY do the trees grow so tall?

Rainforest trees grow very fast in the hot, wet conditions. They race with each other to reach the sun's light, so they grow very tall. Most of them have long, thin trunks. They spread out their branches about 50 metres from the ground to form a leafy **canopy**. But some giant trees, called **emergents**, grow even taller, and tower above the rest of the forest.

Poison dart frog

Many of the smallest animals in the world, such as this tiny chameleon, live in rainforests.

Pygmy chameleon

Over half the known animals and plants in the world live in tropical rainforests!

Rainforests are just like giant sponges. Some of them can soak up a massive ten metres of rain every year!

Scarlet macaw

Colourful macaws and toucans live high in the forest canopy.

WHICH animals live in a rainforest?

An extraordinary variety of animals live in rainforests. They range from biting insects, poisonous frogs and snakes, to butterflies as big as birds, exotic parrots and large **apes**. Animals live at different levels in the trees, depending on where they find their food. Some roam the gloomy forest floor, while others move through the shady **understorey** or spend their whole lives high in the sunny treetops.

Morpho butterflies

Leaf-cutter ants

Now I Know...

★ A rainforest is a forest that grows in hot places where it rains a lot.

★ The trees grow very tall as they reach for sunlight.

★ A huge variety of different animals live in rainforests.

133

Look and Find
★ ★
millipede

WHY is it dark on the forest floor?

It is gloomy down on the floor of the rainforest because very little sunlight filters through the thick canopy of leaves above. It is hot and damp and the air is still. The ground is covered in a layer of dead leaves, tangled roots and young **seedlings**. In fact, it is teeming with millions of insects and tiny creatures.

WHAT are buttress roots?

Giant rainforest trees often have enormous raised roots like wings of wood around the base of their trunks. These are called **buttress roots**. They help to prop up tall trees, just as the buttresses of a cathedral support the cathedral walls.

Poison
dart frog

Army
ants

Tapir

That's Amazing!

Columns of up to 150,000 fierce army ants march across the forest floor, attacking small animals in their way!

Buttress roots can be as tall as a small house!

Tarantula

WHERE do jaguars prowl?

Jaguars are the largest cats in South America and live near rivers deep in the rainforest. They usually hunt at dawn or dusk, when their patterned coats make it hard to spot them prowling through the trees. Jaguars are strong swimmers and catch fish, turtles and even crocodiles. They also climb trees in search of monkeys and sleepy sloths.

Viceroy butterflies

Heliconia flower

Jaguar

Poison dart frog

Now I Know...

★ It is dark on the forest floor as very little sunlight reaches it.

★ Buttress roots prop up tall rainforest trees.

★ Jaguars prowl near rivers in the South American rainforests.

HOW do plants climb trees?

Climbing plants cannot reach the forest canopy by themselves. So they cling onto trees with hooks or **tendrils** and wind their way up around tree trunks towards the sunlight. Giant woody plants called **lianas** loop from one treetop to another and send long roots like ropes back down to the ground.

WHICH vine has poisonous leaves?

The passion flower **vine** has poisonous leaves. Postman caterpillars eat them and become poisonous too, before turning into butterflies. The butterflies' red and black markings warn other animals they are poisonous.

Look and Find ★ ★ cicada

Eyelash viper

Liana

Postman butterfly

Heliconia flower

Passion flower

Poison dart frog

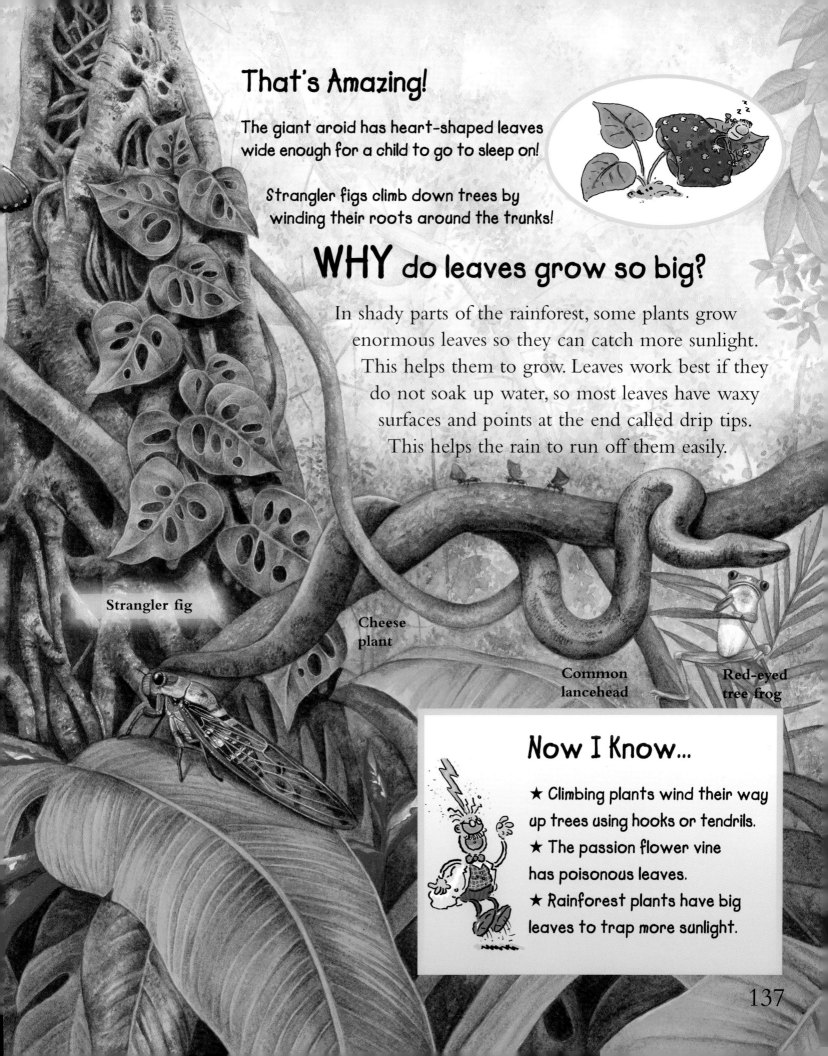

That's Amazing!

The giant aroid has heart-shaped leaves wide enough for a child to go to sleep on!

Strangler figs climb down trees by winding their roots around the trunks!

WHY do leaves grow so big?

In shady parts of the rainforest, some plants grow enormous leaves so they can catch more sunlight. This helps them to grow. Leaves work best if they do not soak up water, so most leaves have waxy surfaces and points at the end called drip tips. This helps the rain to run off them easily.

Strangler fig

Cheese plant

Common lancehead

Red-eyed tree frog

Now I Know...

★ Climbing plants wind their way up trees using hooks or tendrils.
★ The passion flower vine has poisonous leaves.
★ Rainforest plants have big leaves to trap more sunlight.

137

WHO lives in the treetops?

Birds, monkeys, snakes and many other animals live high in the treetops. Here, the branches of the trees lace together to form a huge leafy canopy with plenty of places to shelter and nest. It is hot and sunny, and there are fruit, seeds and leaves to feed on all the year round.

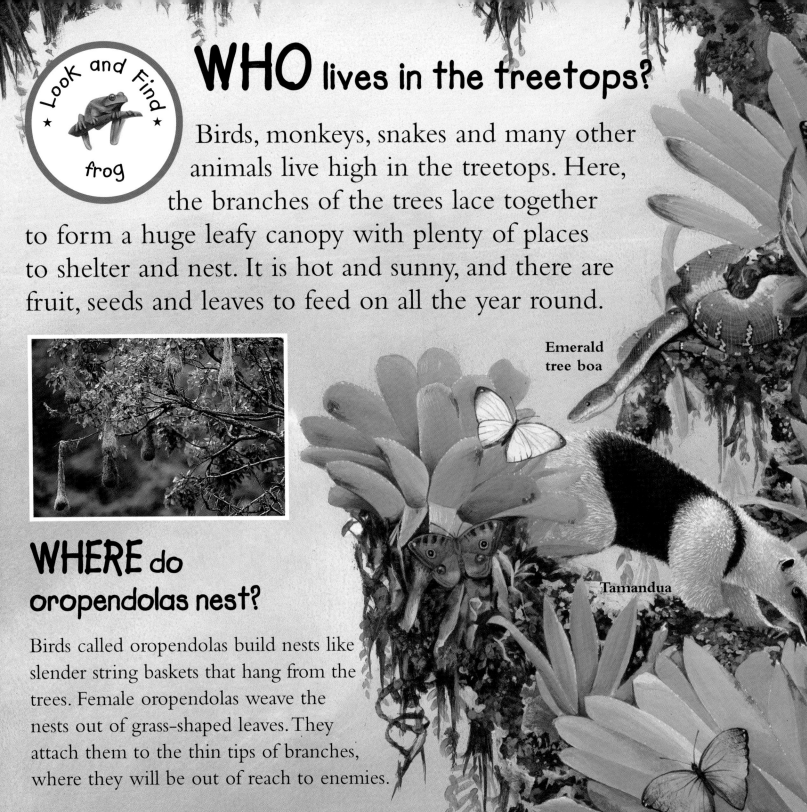

Emerald tree boa

Tamandua

WHERE do oropendolas nest?

Birds called oropendolas build nests like slender string baskets that hang from the trees. Female oropendolas weave the nests out of grass-shaped leaves. They attach them to the thin tips of branches, where they will be out of reach to enemies.

That's Amazing!

The top of a rainforest tree can be as big as a football pitch!

Oropendolas build their nests near wasps' nests to scare off enemies!

138

Harpy eagle

Toucan

Spider monkeys

Sloth

Hummingbird

HOW do spider monkeys cling on to trees?

Spider monkeys use their arms, legs and long, strong tails to cling on to trees. They coil their tails around branches to help them hang on while they pick fruit with their hands. Beneath the tip of the tail is a patch of bare skin like your palm which helps it to grip on to things more tightly.

Now I Know...

★ Birds, monkeys, snakes and many other animals live high in the treetops.

★ Oropendolas build nests that hang from tree branches.

★ Spider monkeys use their tails to cling on to trees.

139

WHAT is an epiphyte?

High above the ground, the branches and trunks of rainforest trees are covered in plants and flowers, like a tropical garden. These plants are called **epiphytes**, or air plants. They cannot grow on the dark forest floor, but thrive high up in the treetops where there is plenty of sunlight. The epiphytes cling to the trees, using their tiny roots as anchors.

That's Amazing!

A really large bromeliad can contain as much as a whole bucketful of water!

More than 28,000 different kinds of epiphytes grow on rainforest trees!

Some flowers, such as **orchids**, are epiphytes too. They often grow in the moss that lives on branches.

HOW do epiphytes catch water?

Epiphytes have many ways of catching water. Some have spongy roots that dangle below branches and absorb water from the air. Others have giant, waxy leaves that funnel rainwater down to their roots. Spiky plants called **bromeliads** have leaves that overlap at the base to form small water tanks. Many plants trap dead leaves to make a damp layer of **compost** in which they can grow.

WHERE do tree frogs hide?

During the hottest part of the day, tiny tree frogs wallow in the small ponds that collect in plants, or they hide beneath damp leaves. Ponds in bromeliads attract plenty of insects for the frogs to eat. Some ponds are deep enough for frogs to lay **frogspawn** during the breeding season.

Now I Know...

★ Epiphytes are plants that grow high in the sunny treetops.
★ Epiphytes absorb water from the air or trap it in leaves.
★ Tree frogs hide in ponds inside plants or under damp leaves.

Look and Find ★ ★ caterpillar

WHAT do hummingbirds eat?

Hummingbirds feed on nectar, a sweet juice found inside flowers. Hummingbirds do not perch on flowers to feed. Instead, they hover in front of them like helicopters, beating their tiny wings up to 90 times a second. This keeps them still enough to push their long beaks into the flowers and suck up the nectar.

That's Amazing!

The rafflesia, the biggest flower in the world, smells like rotting meat!

Bees trapped inside bucket orchids have to follow an obstacle course to escape!

Orchid

HOW do bees help orchids?

Many bees in the rainforest feed on nectar and pollen from orchid flowers. As they visit flowers and gather food, they carry pollen from one flower to another. This helps the orchids to make seeds so more orchids grow.

HOW do plants trap insects?

Pitcher plants trap insects and soak up the **nutrients** from them to get their food. The plants have traps shaped like pitchers or jugs that are half full of liquid. Nectar around the rims of the pitchers attracts insects. They land on the slippery rims, then fall into the liquid inside and drown.

Pitcher plant

Tiger butterfly

Bee

Now I Know...

★ Hummingbirds feed on a juice inside flowers called nectar.
★ Bees carry pollen from one orchid flower to another.
★ Pitcher plants trap insects in their pitchers.

143

WHY do chameleons change colour?

Chameleons are lizards that live in rainforest trees. They camouflage themselves by keeping very still and changing colour to match their surroundings. This makes it hard for insects to see them. Chameleons have hollow, sticky-tipped tongues as long as their bodies and tails. If an insect comes too close, their tongues shoot out and snap them up.

That's Amazing!

Chameleons can swivel their eyes and look in two different directions at once!

South American Indians dip their hunting darts in poison from frogs to make them more deadly!

WHICH frogs are brightly coloured?

Poison dart frogs

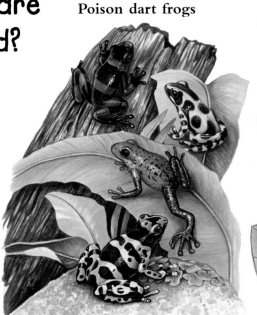

Many rainforest frogs are brightly coloured, but the most colourful of all are poison dart frogs. These tiny frogs are highly poisonous. Their bright colours and patterns act as a warning signal to animals that might eat them, such as snakes.

Camouflaged chameleon

144

Chameleon's long tongue

Reticulated python

HOW does a python hide?

The reticulated python lies without moving amongst the dead leaves on the forest floor. The coloured patterns on its skin help it to blend in with the leaves and camouflage it. The python waits for small animals, frogs and birds to come close. It squeezes its prey to death, before eating them whole.

Now I Know...

★ Chameleons change colour to help them catch food.
★ Poison dart frogs are brightly coloured.
★ The patterns on a python's skin help it hide in dead leaves.

Look and Find ★ ★ basilisk

HOW are rainforests important?

Rainforests are important for many reasons. They are home to plants and animals that live nowhere else in the world. Many everyday foods and things we use, such as coffee, cocoa and rubber, come from rainforest plants. Other plants are used to make life-saving medicines. The huge number of trees in rainforests also affect weather all around the world. Without rainforests, a cold area could become warmer and a dry area could become wetter.

Golden lion tamarins

WHICH animals and plants are endangered?

Rainforests everywhere are being cut down. When this happens, all the plants die and many animals lose their homes and food. Some animals are also killed by hunters or captured and sold as pets. As a result, many plants and animals, from tiny insects to gorillas, are becoming very rare. Some of them, such as the golden lion tamarin, are so rare that they are in danger of dying out altogether.

Morpho butterfly

That's Amazing!

Every year, between 15 and 20 million rainforest animals are smuggled from Brazil and sold as pets!

An area of rainforest about the size of California is destroyed around the world each year!

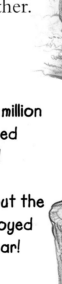

146

WHY are rainforests being destroyed?

Rainforests are destroyed so people can make money from them. Many trees are cut down because their wood is valuable. Huge areas of forest are cut down by companies mining for minerals or oil. Other areas are cleared to make farms. After a few years, the land is like a desert. Nothing else will grow on it, so more forest is cut down.

Coati

Poison dart frog

Now I Know...

★ Rainforests contain valuable plants and animals, and help to control the weather.

★ Many plants and animals are becoming very rare.

★ Forests are cut down for wood, farming and mining.

147

RAINFOREST QUIZ

What have you remembered about the rainforest? Test what you know and see how much you have learned.

1 Where do you find rainforests?
a) in cold places
b) in tropical countries
c) in dry places

2 What lives on the forest floor?
a) monkeys
b) birds
c) insects

3 Which plant has poisonous leaves?
a) strangler fig
b) cheese plant
c) passion flower vine

4 What are epiphytes?
a) plants
b) insects
c) birds

5 What do spider monkeys like to eat?
a) fruit
b) worms
c) birds

6 Which plant traps insects?
a) pitcher plant
b) orchid
c) passion flower vine

7 Where does a reticulated python hide?
a) in the treetops
b) underwater
c) in dead leaves

8 Where do chameleons live?
a) on the ground
b) in trees
c) in ponds

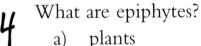

9 What do climbing plants use to cling to trees?
a) vines
b) tendrils
c) leaves

10 Which animal can change colour?
a) chameleon
b) tree frog
c) spider monkey

Find the answers on page 160.

GLOSSARY

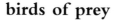

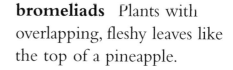

abdomen The lower part of an insect that contains the stomach, and in females produces the eggs.

antennae The sensitive 'feelers' on the head of an insect that are used to touch, taste or smell.

apes Animals like monkeys that do not have tails.

arachnids The group of creepy-crawlies with eight legs, such as spiders and scorpions.

Arctic The cold area around the North Pole.

birds of prey Birds that hunt and kill other animals to eat.

blowhole The nostrils of a whale or dolphin, found on the top of the head.

blubber A thick layer of fat under a sea mammal's skin that keeps it warm.

breach To jump up out of the water and fall back down with a splash.

bromeliads Plants with overlapping, fleshy leaves like the top of a pineapple.

burrows Holes or tunnels in the ground dug and lived in by animals.

buttress roots Roots that form high supports around the bases of tall rainforest trees.

byssus threads The tiny threads with which some molluscs attach themselves to rocks.

camouflage A colour, shape or pattern that hides an object. A **camouflaged** animal looks just like its surroundings, so it is hard to see.

canopy The part of a rainforest where the trees spread out their leafy branches like a high roof.

carcass The dead body of an animal.

carnivores Animals that eat mainly meat.

149

cartilage A light, bendy material that makes up a shark's skeleton. Your ears are made of cartilage.

cells The tiny living units that make up an animal's body.

clutch A group of eggs laid by a bird and incubated together.

cold-blooded Having a body temperature that changes with the surrounding temperature. Reptiles and fish are examples of cold-blooded animals.

colonies Groups of the same type of animal, such as ants, that live and work together in one place.

communicate To pass information, feelings and ideas to others. There are lots of ways of **communicating.** A bird's song, a lion's roar and a chimpanzee's chatter are all ways of using sound to communicate. Some animals use special movements or markings on their bodies to communicate a message or a warning to others.

compost A mixture of dead leaves that is like soil.

compound eyes The type of eyes found in many insects. Each eye is made up of thousands of tiny lenses packed together.

coral reefs Colonies of coral found along tropical shores.

courtship The special way in which animals behave when they are looking for a mate.

creepers Plants that grow along the ground or climb up supports such as trees.

crocodilians A group of reptiles that includes crocodiles, alligators, caimans and gharials.

currents Flows of water or air.

den The hollow home of a wild animal.

digest To break food down into tiny bits that can be used by the body.

driftwood Old, damaged pieces of wood carried onto the seashore by the tides.

echolocation The system used by bats and dolphins to find their way in the dark.

emergents Huge trees that grow taller than the other trees around them in the rainforest.

epiphytes Plants that grow on trees or other plants, instead of in the ground.

estuaries Areas of water where rivers meet the sea.

exoskeleton The outer skeleton of an insect or spider that supports and protects the rest of the body.

fangs Long, sharp, hollow teeth that some snakes use to inject venom into their prey.

filter To separate out food from substances such as water.

frogspawn Frogs' eggs protected by jelly and laid in water.

gills Tiny feather-like parts inside slits behind a fish's or shark's eyes. Fish breathe in oxygen through their gills when water passes over or into them.

glands Parts of the body that make a special substance, such as venom.

glide A bird glides when it sails through the air without flapping its wings.

habitat The natural home of animals or plants. Forests, marshes and grasslands are examples of **habitats.**

hatch To break out of an egg.

herbivores Animals that eat only plants.

hibernating When animals spend several winter months in a deep sleep. In cold areas of the world, hibernation helps many animals to survive the winter.

hollow Not solid.

incubated Kept warm. Eggs are incubated so that chicks or other young can grow inside them.

insectivores Animals that eat only minibeasts.

insects The group of creepy-crawlies that have six legs and three body sections.

invertebrates The group of animals, such as insects and molluscs, without a backbone.

larvae The young of an insect.

lianas Climbing plants with woody stems.

lodge A beaver's home, built from logs and rocks stuck together with mud.

mangrove swamps Soft, wet, tropical coastal land covered in mangrove trees. Mangroves have long, tangled underwater roots that support their trunks above water.

marsupials Mammals, such as kangaroos and koalas, that bring up their young in pouches.

mate When a male and a female of the same kind come together to breed and, as a result, produce young. An animal's partner is called its mate.

metamorphosis When a larva, such as a caterpillar, completely changes its body as it turns into an adult.

migrate To travel from one place to another regularly, usually over long distances, to find food or to mate. Many species make amazingly long **migrations** every year.

molluscs The group of animals, such as slugs and snails, that have soft bodies. Most molluscs' bodies are protected by hard outer shells.

monotremes Mammals that lay eggs rather than giving birth to live young.

moulting Shedding skin, feathers or fur. Insects, spiders and snakes moult by shedding their whole skin before growing into a new one. Birds and mammals lose old, worn-out feathers or fur, and grow new ones in their place.

mucus A slimy fluid produced by many animals, which moistens and protects the body.

nectar The sweet liquid produced by flowers, and eaten by bees and other insects.

nocturnal Busy and active at night rather than during the day.

nourished Looked after and helped to grow. Animals nourish their young by providing them with food and a safe place to grow.

nutrients The useful parts of food that all plants and animals need in order to grow and be healthy.

nymphs Young insects, such as young grasshoppers, that look like tiny copies of their parents.

omnivores Animals that are both meat- and plant-eaters.

orchids Exotic flowers with waxy petals that often grow on rainforest trees. Some orchids are epiphytes.

oxygen A gas found in the air and in water. All animals need to breathe in oxygen to live.

parasites Animals or plants that live on other creatures and are harmful to them. Many animals have parasites that live on their skin.

pellets Balls of undigested food that some birds cough up.

pollen A sticky yellow powder made by flowers. Pollen has to travel or be carried from one flower to another in order for seeds to grow.

predators Animals that hunt other animals for food.

prey Animals that are hunted or killed by other animals.

prides Family groups of lions.

pupae The stage during metamorphosis when young insects change into adults.

153

symbiosis A partnership between two different types of animals which is beneficial to both. An example is the partnership between clown fish and sea anemones.

tags Small plastic labels containing electronic chips that give out signals scientists can follow. Tags are clipped on to sharks' fins – this does not hurt the shark.

talons The long, sharp claws of a bird of prey.

tendrils The small, thread-like parts of climbing plants that reach out to trees and wind themselves around them.

rainforests Thick, tropical forests with very heavy rainfall.

rodents Small mammals with large, sharp front teeth for gnawing.

saliva The watery juice inside an animal's mouth.

scavengers Animals that eat dead or dying fish and animals.

seedlings Young plants that have grown from seeds.

shoal A large group of fish that swims and eats together.

spawn To lay a large number of eggs. Fish and frogs are examples of animals that spawn.

species A particular type of animal or plant.

spiderlings Young spiders.

stranded Washed up and left behind on the seashore.

streamlined Having a smooth body shape that moves easily through air or water.

swim bladder An air-filled organ which helps bony fish to float. Some types of fish also use it for breathing.

territory The area in which an animal lives and hunts.

thorax The middle section of an insect that contains the legs and sometimes the wings.

tide The movement of the sea as it comes high up the seashore and goes out again twice every 24 hours.

tracheae The tiny breathing tubes in an insect.

turf Soil covered in thick, short grass.

understorey The shady, lower part of a rainforest beneath the branches of the trees.

urinates Passes waste liquid, called urine, out of the body.

venom The poison that some snakes and other animals inject into their prey.

vine A tall climbing or trailing plant with long, bendy stems.

viviparous Giving birth to live young. The young develops inside its mother's body, and does not hatch from an egg.

warm-blooded Having a constant body temperature. Mammals and birds are examples of warm-blooded animals.

yolk sac A pouch of thin skin in an egg case that contains yolk, a liquid that provides food for a developing creature.

155

INDEX

D

dancing 81, 102
dens 32, 150
deserts 67, 68–69, 73, 147
digestion 89, 151
dogfish 111
dogs 48
dolphins 34, 35, 49
dormice 42
down feathers 72, 84
dragonflies 11, 13, 23, 42
driftwood 121, 151
drinking 15, 32, 48, 69
ducklings 84

E

eagles 78, 116, 139
earthworms 16, 17
echidnas 47
echolocation 36, 151
egg cases 111, 121
egg teeth 84
eggs 12, 14, 20, 23, 26, 47, 52, 62, 63, 72, 80, 82, 83, 100, 101, 110–111, 114, 116–117, 125
egrets 76
elephants 31, 38, 44–45
emergents 132, 151
endangered species 146
epiphytes 140–141, 151
estuaries 56, 151
exoskeletons 12, 13, 151
eyes 13, 14, 55, 56, 60, 84, 144
eyesight 13, 14, 36, 40, 60, 78, 79

F

fangs 12, 61, 63, 151
fat 33, 42
feathers 72, 73, 84
feet 22, 55, 58, 73, 82
fighting 16, 26, 33
filters 109, 122, 151
fins 92, 96, 98, 105
fireflies 18, 19
fish 57, 59, 85, 92–103, 115, 116, 126, 135
flatfish 99
flies 17, 22
flight 11, 36–37, 72, 74–75, 84
flightless birds 73
flippers 35, 58
flowers 15, 75, 76, 118, 119, 135, 140, 142
flutemouths 92
flying fish 96
flying foxes 36, 37
foxes 116, 119
frigate birds 80
frilled lizards 66
frogs 132, 133, 134, 135, 141, 144
froghoppers 25
frogspawn 141, 151
fur 30

G

gannets 82, 117
garden cross spiders 22
geckos 55, 64
geese 73, 86–87
gharials 57
giant aroids 137
giant tortoises 53
gibbons 132
gila monsters 69
gills 94, 95, 97, 106, 109, 151
giraffes 30, 38, 39
glands 22, 61, 151
gliding 37, 74, 75, 96, 106, 151
glow-worms 18, 19

gobys 92, 103
godwits 124
golden eagles 78–79
golden lion tamarins 146
grass snakes 67
grasses 118, 119
grasshoppers 18, 20–21, 40, 118, 119
great tits 84
great white sharks 106, 108
greenflies 12
grey nurse sharks 110
guillemots 116
gulls 116, 120, 125

H

habitats 24, 68, 151
hagfish 92
hair 12, 19, 22, 30, 32
hammerhead sharks 111
harvest mice 30
hatching 14, 20, 47, 62, 63, 84, 86, 101, 111, 151
hearing 79
heat 68–69, 134
herbivores 38, 151
hermit crabs 126, 129
hibernation 42, 151
hippopotamuses 38, 39
hollows 72, 152
homes 10, 42–43
honeydew 27
honeypot ants 27
horn 73
horse flies 13
hover flies 20
hovering 74, 75, 142
humans 30, 31, 39
hummingbirds 73, 75, 139, 142
hunting 16, 32, 36, 40–41, 56, 60, 64, 78, 79, 98, 104, 105, 146
hunting spiders 12

I

ice 32–33, 114, 115
iguanas 68

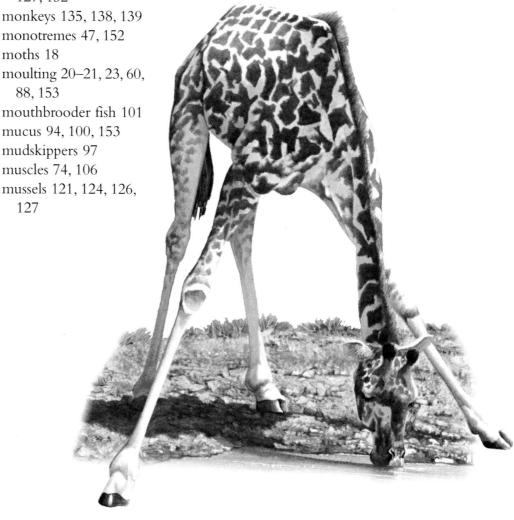

QUIZ ANSWERS

Creepy-crawlies quiz answers: 1c 2a 3c 4c 5c 6a 7a 8b 9b 10b
Mammals quiz answers: 1b 2c 3a 4b 5c 6b 7c 8a 9b 10b
Reptiles quiz answers: 1b 2c 3c 4c 5c 6b 7b 8a 9c 10a
Birds quiz answers: 1c 2b 3c 4b 5a 6c 7a 8b 9b 10b
Fish and Sharks quiz answers: 1c 2a 3a 4c 5a 6b 7b 8c 9c 10c
Seashore quiz answers: 1c 2b 3b 4a 5a 6c 7b 8a 9c 10b
Rainforest quiz answers: 1b 2c 3c 4a 5a 6a 7c 8b 9b 10a